THE SEARCH FOR
EARLY MAN

There are a number of HORIZON CARAVEL BOOKS published each year. Titles now available are:

American Heritage also publishes AMERICAN HERITAGE JUNIOR LIBRARY books, a similar series on American history. Titles now available are:

COVER: *Fifteen thousand years ago man was a cave-dwelling hunter. But he wore clothes and looked much like modern man—as indicated in this recent painting by Maurice Wilson.*

ENDSHEETS: *In another Wilson painting, a man who lived about 250,000 years ago and who was one of our first ancestors joins a pack of wild animals fleeing before a forest fire.*

TITLE PAGE: *Animals, like this bull from a French cave, are a constant theme of early art.*
PHOTO BY ROMAIN ROBERT

A HORIZON CARAVEL BOOK

THE SEARCH FOR
EARLY MAN

By the Editors of
HORIZON MAGAZINE

Author
JOHN E. PFEIFFER

Consultant
CARLETON S. COON

Curator of Ethnology, University Museum, University of Pennsylvania

ILLUSTRATED WITH MANY PAINTINGS, ENGRAVINGS,
AND SCULPTURES FROM PREHISTORIC TIMES

Published by American Heritage Publishing Co., Inc.

Book Trade and Institutional Distribution by Harper & Row

FIFTH PRINTING
Library of Congress Catalogue Card Number: 63–16371
© 1968 by American Heritage Publishing Co., Inc., 551 Fifth Avenue, New York, New
York, 10017. All rights reserved under Berne and Pan-American Copyright Conventions.
Trademark CARAVEL registered United States Patent Office

C.N.M.H., PARIS

FOREWORD

In September, 1940, four boys were walking along a narrow plateau high above the Vézère River in war-torn France. Their dog was lost; he seemed to have disappeared into the earth. The boys examined a hole where a washout had uprooted a pine tree—perhaps he had gone down there. They slithered into the hole and found themselves in a rock chamber covered with enormous painted animals. They had discovered the Lascaux cave, which is now famed throughout the world for murals that had remained hidden from men's eyes for more than eighteen thousand years.

This book tells the story of Lascaux and of the prehistoric people who came there to worship by torchlight as the magic paintings were made. It tells of many other caves in the same part of France where different kinds of art works and weapons have been found from eras even more ancient. And it shows the richness of these objects in photographs and in retrospective paintings.

Many of the paintings are pure guesswork—artists trying to imagine the faces of our ancestors from no more evidence than a few fossilized bones. Others are based on painstaking research into the flora and fauna of prehistoric times.

Archaeology, the science of digging into the past, is now seeking to eliminate much of the guesswork, but none of the excitement, from prehistory. Two of the most important sites for that rugged work are located near Lascaux. These "digs" are described in close-up detail by this book's author, who has been there and has explored the sites in person.

The distant past is still mysterious, and the search for early man is only beginning. Anthropologists have long known that our ancestors were hunters and warriors—but have we inherited any peaceable characteristics as well? The answer may lie in the cave paintings and in the prehistoric living patterns that are now being investigated. Perhaps the two greatest challenges to a new generation of scientists are the discovery of man's place in furthest space and his cultural origins in remotest time.

THE EDITORS

This fierce black bull is one of several hundred animals on the walls of the Lascaux cave. Prehistorians believe the paintings had a magic purpose.

The first drawing in which apes and men appeared together was this unscientific illustration from the 1598 journal of an Italian traveler in Africa.

CONTENTS

I

THE VALLEY OF CAVES

In the southwestern part of France, over three hundred miles from Paris, lies a deep little valley with a trail running down each side. Recently I investigated the valley, following one of the trails through the woods to the edge of a field. Across the field, perched high on a gray limestone cliff, was a ruined castle with three towers. My wife and I, our son, and a friend of his gazed at the castle through the summer haze; it was here that we hoped to find a work of art made by men more than fifteen thousand years ago.

This castle was the medieval fortress of Commarque, where our search would begin. Less than two weeks before, a professor of prehistory had told me that beneath the castle, at the bottom of the cliff, I would find a small cave in which was an incredibly ancient masterpiece. "The cave runs about ninety feet into the cliff and is T-shaped," he had said. "In the right-hand gallery of the T you'll find the engraving—a horse's head, viewed in profile. There's nothing quite like it anywhere. But there will be no guide, so be sure to take your own lights. To get there you'll have to follow the path half a mile or so across the field."

With the encouragement of a farmer who waved us on from a distance, we followed the path. Partly overgrown, it passed over marshy ground through tall grass, purple flowers, and clumps of nettles. We reached the foot of the cliff and started looking for the cave, first wandering into a number of the castle's damp chambers: a medieval stable, a room that might once have served as a wine cellar, a place for storing wood and farm implements. All these basement rooms were hewed out of the limestone cliff. Finally we

The rich cave area of southern France has yielded many clues to an understanding of prehistoric people. Left, the Dordogne River is seen from the mouth of a cave dwelling. At right is a human skull found in earth layers.

*Beneath the medieval castle of Commarque,
at left, lies the cave where the author
searched for the engraving of a horse's
head, pictured at right. It was carved
in the Magdalenian period, about 15,000
years ago, with a tool like the one above.*

found the cave itself at the back of a natural recess, or
shelter, where an ancient river had once cut into the cliff
making a hollowed-out overhang.

Then we started a second search that almost turned
out to be fruitless, the search for the prehistoric engraving.
The entrance to the cave was an ample hole about six feet
high leading into a small vault; the two galleries, or wings,
forming the top of the T ran right and left at the end of the
vault. There seemed to be no danger of getting lost. The
right-hand gallery, the one the professor had specified as
the location of the engraving, extended for no more than
seventy-five feet or so. In most places the gallery was wide
enough to walk through without much trouble except at the
very end where it narrowed and the roof slanted down
sharply. There we had to sidle through and crawl along
on hands and knees.

Even though the cave was small and our directions
were exact, we had a difficult time finding the engraving.
In fact, a trained anthropologist had recently looked for
it in vain; when he heard that we were also planning to
look, he implied that since he had not succeeded, we might
as well give up. Naturally, that made us more determined
than ever.

The problem here at Commarque, and also at many

The Beginnings of Art, GIEDION, 1962

A frieze of eight engraved horses was carved in limestone at Cap Blanc. A close-up photograph of the frieze is at left; a recent oil painting of it appears below.

other caves containing prehistoric art, is that the engravings may not consist of deeply incised lines that stand out to the eye. As we learned eventually, the lines of these engravings are often fairly shallow, and the flat surfaces have the same muddy gray-brown color as the rest of the rock. When you try to see them you are operating under adverse conditions. It is not possible to step back and survey a large area of wall, since the passage itself may be a mere two or three feet wide, or less in many cases. Since the ceilings may be low, you are lucky indeed if you can even manage to stand up straight. Also, you tend to imagine things in caves and may mistake natural patterns of lines and cracks for man-made patterns.

We looked and looked for the elusive engraving. The four of us squeezed past one another in the right-hand gallery, shining our flashlights over the walls and ceiling and carefully examining every line that seemed promising. About halfway along the gallery we found an engraving of a small horse, and at the end of the corridor we spotted the outline of a vaguely depicted animal and a form that might have been a bear's head. Occasionally, one of us would feel convinced that a pattern of lines represented "something," only to be talked out of it by the skeptical comments of the rest of the group.

After more than half an hour of searching, I began to have doubts. Perhaps there had been some mistake. Perhaps I had misunderstood the professor and he had referred me to the left-hand, not the right-hand, gallery. So I shifted my quest to that gallery. Not long afterward I heard a shout, from the other gallery of course: "I've found it!" We all rushed to the spot.

At first I could see nothing. I tried hard, but there was only an apparently featureless expanse of gray wall. It was my son's friend who had recognized the profile of the horse's head. He pointed: "See, there's the nostril." And all at once the entire head, beautifully executed in low relief and plain as day, appeared as if it had suddenly been placed before my eyes at that very moment—neck, cheek, eye, ear, and mane. Long long ago an artist had indicated the mane by a series of lightly engraved lines colored a reddish brown. He had selected natural indentations or pockmarks in the wall to represent the nostril pit and had used a naturally curved, raised portion of the rock to represent the swelling cheekbone.

It was an amazing experience to draw an utter blank at first, and then given a clue (the flaring nostril), to see the whole picture clear and almost alive in the half-light coming from the side. Moreover, before my son's friend brought our search to a successful conclusion, we had all played our lights over the same part of the wall and had missed the engraving completely. That ended our excursion except for one thing more. My son sifted through some loose dirt not far from the picture and found a curved flint blade worn at the pointed end—an engraving tool. Perhaps it was one of the tools the artist had used to make the horse's head.

This then was a search for one tangible piece of history, or rather prehistory—the study of man before there were written records. I had undertaken the search knowing that the horse's head was but a small part of the whole story of early man. Similarly, my route into the valley—down the path and across the field, into the cave and up to the en-

Early man made his home in caves formed beneath natural limestone overhangs. At right is a typical cave opening in a cliff. Above is a part of the Laussel shelter; at far right is the recently built entrance to the Cap Blanc site.

graving itself—was but a tiny red line on the surface of a large regional map (see page 28).

The region is so rich in the cave dwellings of early man that it could be called the Valley of Caves. Through it flows the Vézère River, where our expedition began, and in the valley there are also many other rivers and side valleys. Throughout the world this region is known for the prehistoric sites that have been discovered there. And the castle at Commarque is by no means the region's most extraordinary site. Directly across that little valley is the sixteenth-century château of Laussel, near which, hidden by bushes, is the Laussel rock shelter. There, on the 350-yard-wide terrace that overlooks the valley and is protected by the overhanging cliff, was found a series of five limestone blocks with crude human figures etched into them. They were low relief (raised and slightly three-dimensional) carvings of a man, three women, and a man and a woman together made by an artist at a time much earlier than the Commarque horse.

Not far away are two other sites. The trail that we had taken into the valley has a fork in it. If we had gone straight ahead instead of turning left into the field, we would have reached another rock shelter called Cap Blanc. Here more than fifty years ago an investigator examined the wall; noticing deep incisions filled with earth, he picked up a stick and knocked the earth away. He discovered a low-relief frieze of eight horses, and later he found the skeleton of a woman buried at the foot of the frieze. We went to Cap Blanc and then on to the small cave of la Grèze, which has a large engraving of a bison. The cave also has an intriguing, narrow side-tunnel which we crawled into, but our way was then blocked by a wall of earth.

The valley of the Vézère thus contains not one site but a cluster of sites, and many more lie close by. There is another lovely valley about five miles away where prehistoric men are known to have lived hundreds of centuries before the Pyramids were built. It is the valley of Castel Merle, which branches off the Vézère. You walk along a strip of meadow at the bottom of a kind of chasm. One side slopes gently upward, with trees and undergrowth and then a row of rock shelters, terraces in the slope protected by overhanging limestone. The other side of the chasm is steep. The trees and undergrowth here are much thicker; you have to scramble and make a path through branches and vines to get at the sites hidden far above.

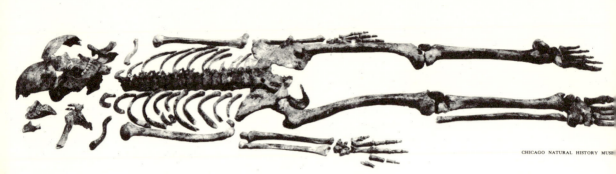

Another clue to the existence of prehistoric people besides their art is the burial of their dead. These carefully layed out bones, the skeleton of a young girl, were found beneath the horse frieze at the Cap Blanc site.

Carved horses have been found under one of the limestone overhangs. These horses were done in the same style as those at Cap Blanc and were originally in low relief, but time and the weather have all but obliterated them. This isolated valley of Castel Merle contains a total of sixteen known sites, eight of which have been excavated at one time or another. In the stillness of the valley you wonder about the sort of communities that once existed here.

The river that runs through the valley was higher and broader in prehistoric times. Women must have shouted to one another from their rock shelters, exchanging gossip and keeping an eye on the children playing in the meadows by the river. Perhaps hunters returning near the end of the day discussed new strategies, compared kills, boasted, described the big ones that got away. And at night what were the feelings of the cliff dwellers as they saw the lights of neighbors' fires on the hillside across the way?

Of course, not all the people of the valley lived there at the same time. Art found on the walls of caves and rock shelters is the work of men essentially like ourselves. These creative people, with whom we cannot help but feel a bond, moved into the shelters about two hundred and fifty centuries ago. And the shelters they found had been occupied in an even earlier time by a more primitive type of man.

Just a few miles farther up the valley of the Vézère is the most famous prehistoric site of all, the Lascaux cave with its galleries of engravings and magnificent color paintings. Lascaux was brought to light only two decades ago when four boys went walking on a wooded plateau three hundred feet above the left bank of the river. Their dog disappeared down a hole where a storm had uprooted a pine tree. The boys slid down into the hole and found the galleries, and the dog. The cave is still being excavated, but that hole is not the original entrance. The opening that the ancient cave dwellers used and defended has not yet been found. The Lascaux cave, with its brilliant walls and ceilings, originally served as a religious gathering place. Today, as a place to visit and marvel at, it ranks with the greatest

TEXT CONTINUED ON PAGE 23

This bison engraving was found on a wall at la Grèze cave. It was done by an Aurignacian artist about the same time as the venus opposite.

In prehistoric art a carving of a woman is generally called a venus. At left is the famous Venus of Laussel, a seventeen-inch-high woman holding a bison horn. The figure was found on the overhang of a limestone shelter.

19

THE SACRED ANIMALS OF LASCAUX

The most splendid examples of Paleolithic art are the paintings at the Lascaux cave in the Vézère Valley in France. Since there is no evidence that men actually lived in the cave, it was probably used as a religious shrine about 17,000 years ago. The figures adorning the walls are considered to have been sacred symbols. At right is a general view of the Great Hall of Bulls, and lower right is a detail of a bull's head. The frieze of ponies seen below decorates one wall of the narrow Axial Gallery—a corridor leading from the Great Hall.

21

TIME CHART OF THE WORLD'S GROWTH

PALEOZOIC						MESOZOIC	
CAMBRIAN	ORDOVICIAN	SILURIAN	DEVONIAN	CARBONIFEROUS	PERMIAN	TRIASSIC	JURASSIC
600,000,000 years ago	500,000,000		400,000,000	300,000,000		200,000,000	

PLEISTOCENE EPOCH

Lower Paleolithic	Middle

First Glacial   Second Glacial   Third Glacial

600,000 — 540,000   480,000 — 380,000   240,000 — 180,000

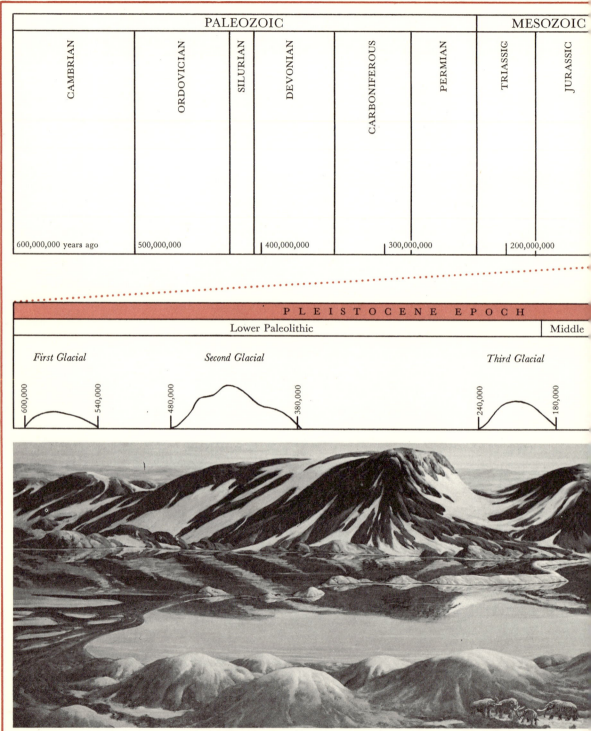

The Pleistocene epoch's glaciers shaped Europe's face (above). The epoch is divided into the Paleolithic periods of man's

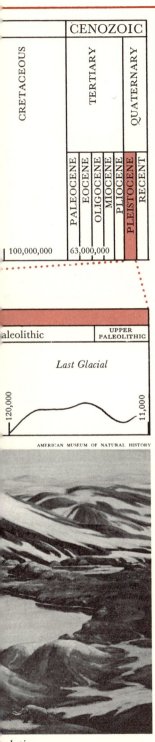

CENOZOIC		
CRETACEOUS	TERTIARY	QUATERNARY

	PALEOCENE	EOCENE	OLIGOCENE	MIOCENE	PLIOCENE	PLEISTOCENE	RECENT

100,000,000   63,000,000

aleolithic	UPPER PALEOLITHIC

Last Glacial

120,000   11,000

olution.

TEXT CONTINUED FROM PAGE 19

museums and cathedrals of modern French history—the Louvre, Chartres, and Notre Dame.

The sites that I have mentioned are only a few of the caves and rock shelters in the Valley of Caves. The center of the entire region, the village of les Eyzies, lies fifteen miles downstream from Lascaux, just above the junction of the Vézère and Dordogne rivers. A huge cliff that looms over the village has a long record of its own. Ten to thirty thousand years ago the people who painted and engraved on rock walls settled in the high shelters of the cliff. And forty to fifty thousand years ago—long before the cave painters—another people occupied the shelters. These earlier men were different from us and from the relatively modern cave dwellers. They were more limited and less intelligent; if they had art, we have not discovered it. They are now known as Neanderthal men.

As the Neanderthals lived, worked, and died they deposited new layers of dirt and refuse on top of old layers. Then the new people came and added their refuse. These "living floors" eventually served as foundations for a castle built into the cliff by feudal lords during the tenth and eleventh centuries. The ruins of this castle have been rebuilt into the les Eyzies Museum of Prehistory.

Now imagine rising in a helicopter along the steep side of the cliff and hovering up above, high enough for a birds'-eye view of the Valley of Caves. You see where the Vézère River winds its way past cliffs and rolling meadows and forests, where it rushes through the town of les Eyzies, joins the Dordogne, and empties into the Bay of Biscay near Bordeaux. You are looking down on an amazing concentration of prehistory. Within a radius of about twenty-five miles of les Eyzies there are more than a hundred and fifty prehistoric sites—that is, known sites.

The number of undiscovered treasures may well be two or three times greater. There are no reliable estimates, but one observation suggests that the region has not been

If the history of life on earth, beginning with the first evidence of marine life, were presented in a year-long motion picture, modern man would appear only during the last eleven minutes. Life began 600,000,000 years ago in the Cambrian period (see chart, left) when marine creatures appeared. Fishes appeared during the Ordovician, amphibians during the Devonian, reptiles during the Carboniferous, and dinosaurs first during the Triassic period. Mammalian life began in the Jurassic and flourished during the Cretaceous but was not noticeably abundant until the Eocene period.

23

There was a period of 150,000,000 years between the appearance of the am-
phibious dinosaurs (like the huge brontosaurus pictured above) and the land-
roving woolly mammoth (below) of the Paleolithic era, or Old Stone Age.
By the end of the Paleolithic era man had fully evolved. Below left, dinosaur bones are uncovered at the Dinosaur National Monument in Utah.

explored exhaustively. Detailed maps show that the great majority of known sites lie within a mile or so of established routes, automobile roads and old-time carriage roads. You get a feeling for what could be discovered when you drive up out of a well-explored valley, stop at the top of a high hill, and see in the near distance a green and tempting valley—and beyond that another valley, and another still farther beyond.

You realize that there is much to be found and that it would take many days of hiking and nights of camping to find it. The maps confirm your impression. They reveal several out-of-the way valleys which do not have a single mark indicating the location of a site. Specialists in the study of prehistory are not likely in the near future to lead large-scale expeditions into the back country. They have far too much work on their hands right now in attempting, often with inadequate funds, to explore some of the known sites. One investigator told me that excavating the sites by modern techniques would require some two hundred trained persons working for at least fifty years.

As far as clues to the character of early man are concerned, this is one of the richest regions in the world. It

BOTH: CHARLES R. KNIGHT: PRINCETON UNIVERSITY MUSEUM OF NATURAL HISTORY

was a kind of prehistoric Manhattan, with les Eyzies as the Times Square. People of the remote past came to the valley and stayed for long periods. Here they found a little world made to order for them, preparations having been started more than a hundred million years ago during the time when dinosaurs roamed the earth. Then in the Western Hemisphere great seas covered more than half of North America, and volcanic upheavals were forming the Rocky Mountains. During this Cretaceous period in Europe, seas covered most of the Continent, including France.

The region around les Eyzies had long been submerged in the waters at the edge of the deepest seas. In quiet warm lagoons creatures such as jellyfish and sea anemones developed stony skeletons, and in dying left heaps of their bodies in the form of coral reefs. After millions of years the waters receded and exposed the reefs, huge masses of solid limestone. Rivers like the Vézère and the Dordogne cut deep channels through the limestone, forming steep cliffs with curving basins and overhangs. And here, ages later, prehistoric man found shelters and caves everywhere, natural homes carved in the limestone.

He also found ample supplies of drinking water—and raw materials. Imbedded in the limestone, like nuts in a nougat, were lumps of flint which could be worked into tools and weapons. How the flint became concentrated into lumps is still something of a mystery, but most geologists believe that the flint, like the limestone itself, was deposited by living things.

Besides flint and water, the most important thing that man found in the region was game—plentiful and easy to capture. During the era of prehistoric man in Europe, and for a long time before that, the Continent had an unprecedented number of all sorts of animals. Into western Europe deer, bison, and horses migrated from eastern Europe and Asia; hippopotamuses, rhinoceroses, and elephants from the warm plains of northern Africa and southern Asia; chamois and ibex from the Alps, Pyrenees, Caucasus, and Urals; antelopes and horses from the steppes and deserts of eastern Europe and central Asia; reindeer and woolly mammoths and rhinoceroses from the tundras and barren lands of arctic territories. The region surrounding les Eyzies in particular seems to have been a kind of crossroad for the seasonal migrations of huge herds of reindeer, which, as we shall see, provided our ancestors with one of their most dependable sources of food.

So prehistoric man, the latest and most advanced of

When the Valley of Caves was below sea level in the Cambrian period, marine creatures (above) lived there and shed their skeletons. Heaped together, millions of these formed reefs, and as the water receded, the reefs became exposed limestone hills. Later, glaciers and rivers bored through the limestone, forming cliffs and rock shelters. At right, the town of les Eyzies huddles at the base of one such cliff.

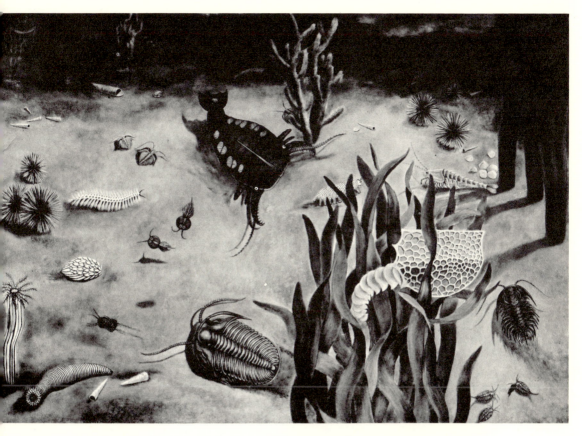

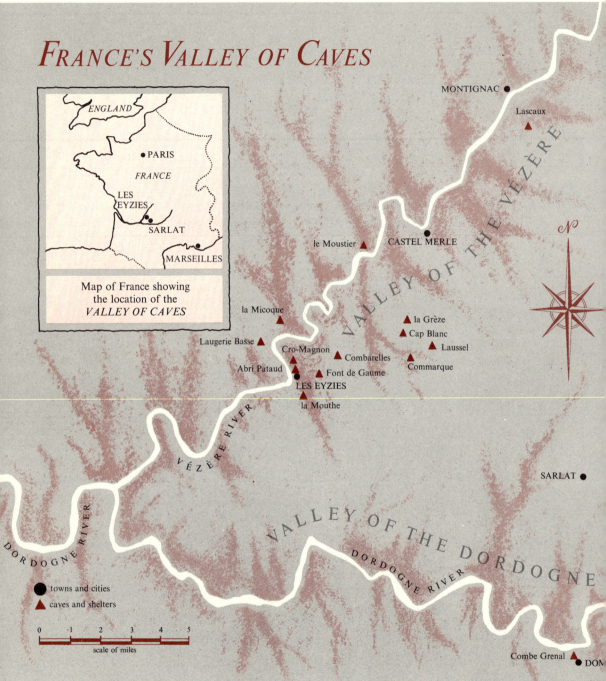

FRANCE'S VALLEY OF CAVES

MONTIGNAC ●

Lascaux ▲

VALLEY OF THE VÉZÈRE

N

Map inset

ENGLAND

● PARIS

FRANCE

LES
EYZIES

SARLAT

MARSEILLES

**Map of France showing
the location of the
*VALLEY OF CAVES***

le Moustier ▲   CASTEL MERLE ●

VALLEY OF THE VÉZÈRE

la Micoque ▲

▲ la Grèze

▲ Cap Blanc

Laugerie Basse ▲

▲ Laussel

Cro-Magnon ▲

Abri Pataud

▲ Combarelles

▲ Commarque

LES EYZIES ●

▲ Font de Gaume

▲ la Mouthe

VÉZÈRE RIVER

SARLAT ●

VALLEY OF THE DORDOGNE

DORDOGNE RIVER

DORDOGNE RIVER

● towns and cities

▲ caves and shelters

0   1   2   3   4   5

scale of miles

Combe Grenal ▲

● DOM

*In the valleys of the Dordogne and Vézère rivers are many prehistoric cave
sites—so many that the author has called the entire region the Valley of
Caves (above). At bottom right is Combe Grenal, a Neanderthal site where
an excavation discussed in Chapter IV is now in progress. Clustered around
the village of les Eyzies are a number of Upper Paleolithic shelters. Les
Eyzies' geographical location is shown on the map of France at top left.*

the mammals, joined the mass migration and found here a rare combination of abundant water, flint, and game. But the region was probably popular for other reasons—for example, its beautiful scenery. After all, we no longer depend on hunting or on caves and rock shelters; yet the same region which attracted early man still attracts so many tourists that hotels and rooming houses are booked solid months in advance. Perhaps temperament and esthetic appreciation, as well as more practical considerations, helped to determine the choice of a place to live even during the rigorous conditions of times past. Perhaps early man was deeply aware of what he was doing when he moved into the Valley of Caves and found there a fortunate environment.

In any case, an extraordinary process was under way, a process that seemed to speed up as great glaciers moved south across the face of Europe. New breeds of men were shaped, and their offspring spread with increasing rapidity. The process involved an interplay of complex and subtly related forces: the Valley of Caves was one focus of these intensive and dramatic changes. Commarque, Laussel, Cap Blanc, la Grèze, Lascaux, and many other sites of the region provide records of the earliest-known art and tantalizing hints as to how the artists may have lived and worked. There are now museums full of worked flint and bone, skeletal remains, relics, and artifacts in France and in other countries of the world.

An enormous amount remains to be learned, however. In fact, no prehistorian alive today expects that he will live long enough to find complete answers to the most crucial questions confronting him. This is definitely a job for the future. Although sites in and around les Eyzies have been excavated for more than a century, in an important sense the scientific research is just beginning. Workers are using new methods with a new precision; they are experimenting with techniques that have yet to prove themselves. The study of prehistory is a new and expanding branch of science which calls for the cooperation of many specialists—anthropologists, geologists, zoologists, botanists, chemists, and physicists.

Our story centers about the town of les Eyzies and the Valley of Caves. But the story cannot be fully appreciated without an understanding of what was happening in times and places even more remote. These inquiries into the nature of man's predecessors and origins are taken up in the next chapter, which concerns the evolution of man in Africa.

PIERRE LAURENT

Above, an early man makes a stone tool. During the Paleolithic era early men moved into France's Valley of Caves because of the ample supply of water, flint, and game. Sketches like this are based on recent ideas of early man's appearance.

II

APE MEN OF AFRICA

In 1766 a French naturalist dared link men with apes by drawing an almost human-looking chimpanzee.

We took an imaginary helicopter flight in the preceding chapter, hovering over les Eyzies to view the entire region spread out like a map below. The invention that would help us most in the next stage of our story does not exist except in science fiction, but we will assume that there is such a thing. It is a time machine which can stay put in space, hanging steadily over the same region, and which can travel backward in time. The landscape becomes younger and younger as we look down. In effect we see a motion picture running quickly in reverse from the present to historic and then to prehistoric days. Every minute of watching takes us a thousand years further back into the past.

The most striking changes come soonest. The immediate past vanishes abruptly, within the first ten seconds. The valley's tourist shops and restaurants vanish, along with the other traces and trappings of modern times: hotels, automobiles, garages, black-topped roads, overhead power lines, telephone and telegraph wires, fences, railroad tracks. One by one all things familiar to us are erased from the scene, and we begin to realize how very recent our way of life is. The nineteenth and twentieth centuries have passed; the landscape is suddenly less cluttered.

There are appearances, brief ones, as well as disappearances during the next minute or so. Buildings buried or in ruins today are reassembled before our eyes. Fragmented stones, rotted rafters, and the decayed straw of thatched roofs become peasants' homes again. Some of the houses take shape like growing plants in the hollows of rock shelters, only to fade almost as soon as they come into being. Ruined châteaux and castles are transformed in the

TEXT CONTINUED ON PAGE 34

The head of Rhodesian man has been rendered by an artist from a 23,000-year-old skull. Other human bones from Africa may be 2,000,000 years old.

Nearly two million years ago Africa's plains swarmed with strange animals. Above the saber-toothed

tiger at left are prehistoric pigs, sheep, and elephants. Baboons and manlike apes run beside the lake.

TEXT CONTINUED FROM PAGE 31

same way. The crumbling medieval fortress of Commarque, for example, returns to its former splendor, and
pennants wave for a while on its tower. Then the castle
vanishes, and the limestone cliff is covered with trees.

Soon we see nothing that bears the mark of man. We
are moving too swiftly into the past to see changing seasons or knights in armor or bands of hunters going in and
out of caves and shelters. Their man-centered world passes
in half an hour. From now on nature takes over, and we
merely observe for long periods as things happen on a
grand scale. Pine forests, snow fields, and tundras give way
to tropical landscapes and then fitfully reappear during the
advances and recessions of the great glaciers.

Finally it is time to stop. After traveling more than
thirty hours at a millennium-per-minute rate, we press an
appropriate button in our time machine and bring the
flash-back process to a halt. Now we are looking down on
the Valley of Caves as it existed long long ago—a lush,
moist countryside of temperate climate and perpetual summer. Dense rain forests include sassafras, sumac, locust,
cypress, and tulip trees, and perhaps some bamboo palms.
Elephants, horses, deer, and cattle graze in meadows scattered like islands among the forests; saber-toothed tigers
stalk through tall grasses; monkeys and gibbonlike apes live
in trees along the edges of the meadows. We may even see
an occasional hippopotamus wallowing in the mud of the
ancient Dordogne and Vézère rivers.

Life flourishes, but the loneliness has a nightmare
quality. It is far deeper and more frightening than any-
one living today could possibly imagine. You might get
a faint idea of how it must have been by camping out
alone in a Canadian forest or in the Amazon jungles. But
that would not be the same thing. Here there is no
possibility of walking out of the forest into civilization.
If our time machine broke down we would be terribly
isolated, stranded in a world without human beings.
Furthermore, this is a world that is changing for the
worse: if we were marooned in this land of more than
a million years ago, we would be faced with a major
climate change. We would not be able to see the first
signs of change from our viewing point. But in high
places among the Alps, glaciers are beginning to form,
and the snow line is creeping lower and lower. And to
the north along the southeast coast of England, not far
from the present-day locations of London and the white
cliffs of Dover, chill currents are coming from the Arctic

Two evolutionary stages between ape and man are shown below: at right is a vaguely manlike ape, and at left is an upright ape man.

34

A short-necked giraffe, the siv-
athere (left), existed in Africa
during the Pleistocene epoch but
is now extinct. Its antlers resembled those of the modern moose.

Ocean. These deep-flowing waters foreshadow the Ice Age. Soon, geologically speaking, the monkeys and apes will disappear. These animals, resembling man's earliest ancestors so closely, will vanish from the forest's edges; they will become extinct or migrate south across the Mediterranean via the land bridge of Sicily.

Because of the massively destructive glaciers, no traces of the first manlike inhabitants of earth can be found in the Valley of Caves or in France, or in any part of Europe. With our machine we have reached the right time but the wrong place. To see man's ancestors we must move south like the apes, using our time machine as a conventional-style aircraft. We fly more than three thousand miles to East Africa, to an entirely different type of countryside in Tanganyika, south of Lake Victoria. We look down on a wide, scorched plain that is only beginning to reforest itself. In the near distance steam hisses from still-active volcanoes whose peaks rise ten thousand feet above sea level. This is the site we have been looking for—a certain part of Africa, nearly two million years ago.

The climate has been dry, but tropical rains have begun. Large ferns, acacia trees, and other tropical plants thrust up from the plain, making an open tropical woodland. Ponds and swampy areas are scattered over the uneven lava floor, and the dominant feature of the landscape is a lake twenty miles long with a few small green islands. Among the wildlife there are varieties of such familiar things as gazelles, elephants, crocodiles, and tigers. But there are also some very peculiar animals: pigs the size of rhinoceroses, sheep six feet tall, giraffes with broad moose-like antlers, baboons bigger than gorillas.

The strange menagerie also includes another, less spectacular, type of animal. He attracts our attention because we know about coming events and have a special interest in this animal's future. A troop of hairy creatures rest on the slopes of a rocky hill overlooking the plain and the lake. They look and behave very much like baboons or chimpanzees, squatting on the grass, grooming one an-other in pairs, scuffling watchfully from place to place. Suddenly one of them catches sight of something that

Dr. Louis Leakey points across Olduvai Gorge. The floor of the gorge is the plain where some of the world's first ape men once roamed. It has been exposed by fissures and rivers that cut through layers of silt deposited in more recent times. Above is a map of Africa that locates Olduvai.

signifies danger. With a sharp cry the creature stands erect and walks awkwardly for a few steps and then starts to run. In his right hand he carries a stone.

Our search has ended—we have seen an upright primate, a member of the order that includes monkeys, apes, and men. Like man this upright animal has the sense to use weapons.

The scene we have witnessed by means of an imaginary time machine has actually been reconstructed by scientists working from a mass of evidence painstakingly accumulated over many years. In the absence of time machines, these prehistorians have had to work from facts and shrewd deductions rather than by direct observations. A great deal remains to be learned, and they may never discover some of the things they want most to know. But the piecing together of evidence goes on, and new excavations and studies are revealing more and more about the complex course of human evolution.

A major phase of this investigation is currently under way in Africa. Here investigators have found fossils of the oldest-known apes and also of the oldest-known creatures that were something more than apes. Where did these superior apes come from? No one knows. Their precise ancestry may go back four million years or more when vast areas which had been rich forests turned semiarid and trees became scarce; many tree dwellers adapted to these changes by coming down to the ground.

But we do know a good deal else about them: what they looked like and what they could do. Evidence was left for us on the Tanganyika plain. But the evidence lies buried beneath the deposits of the ages, three hundred feet of earth and rock. There it might have remained forever if nature had not obligingly done an excavating job for us. The raging waters of African rivers cut through the sand and sediment down to the lava floor, gouging a Y-shaped system of steep chasms—and exposing thick geologic layers and their contents.

This miniature Grand Canyon, known as the Olduvai Gorge, is the world's richest and most remarkable site for discoveries from earliest prehistoric times. It is the archaeological headquarters of Louis Leakey and his wife Mary, investigators associated with the Coryndon Museum in Nairobi, Kenya. For thirty years off and on they worked together in the isolated gorge, with limited funds and with little attention except from a few fellow specialists.

However, the hard-scrabble conditions under which the

Dr. Leakey compares the jawbone of a modern man with the recently found jawbone of an ape believed to be an ancient ancestor of humans. He may have existed 14,000,000 years ago in the Miocene epoch.

Leakeys had been working have changed for the better—largely because of a discovery made one July morning in 1959. While examining a slope where the gorge divides into two branches, Mary Leakey noticed a bit of fossilized bone lying in rocky debris, and higher on the slope she came upon two fossilized teeth. She immediately recognized that these objects were something out of the ordinary. Nineteen days of careful excavating yielded more than a hundred major fragments which have been fitted together jigsaw style into an almost complete skull, with only the lower jaw missing.

Immediately the Leakeys went to work. The question uppermost in their minds was, was this skull that of an ape—or a man—or an ape man? The teeth alone, sixteen beautifully preserved uppers, provided vital details. Their size and stage of development indicated that they belonged to a male sixteen to eighteen years old—which would make the creature fairly young by present-day standards. Actually, however, he was well past his middle age: recent studies have shown that these ancient beings had a life span of only twenty-five years or so.

This ancient, teen-aged ape man was a formidable animal—he had a massive jaw with huge molars and special bony ridges on the skull where extra-powerful jaw muscles were attached. Louis Leakey gave him an equally formidable name, *Zinjanthropus boisei*. *Zinjanthropus* is a composite Arabic-Greek word meaning "East Africa man"; *boisei* was chosen to commemorate an Englishman, Charles Boise, who has helped the National Geographic Society support work at the Olduvai Gorge. The ape man's name is too much of a mouthful even for scientists, and to experts and laymen he is known simply as Zinj.

Perhaps Zinj was merely a gorilla. His heavy cranium housed a relatively small brain about the size of an orange and weighing a pound or so—which falls well within the range of gorilla brains. By contrast, a modern man's brain averages three pounds. But Zinj walked erect and used his hands in a new way. Crude tools were found with his remains, mostly water-worn rocks of about the right size and shape to fit snugly into the hand. These are not objects picked up and used as is, the way an ape or a monkey would use them. They are deliberately worked and shaped according to a simple pattern. The rocks have been sharpened along one edge; on both sides of the edge, pieces, or flakes, have been chipped off. Thus Zinj made choppers for his own purposes. For killing, he also used various bashing

The important fossil skull found by Dr. Leakey is seen here under a reconstruction of Zinj's head. The flat cranium held a brain about one third the size of modern man's.

stones. Furthermore, he probably ate more meat than any known ape, past or present; we can deduce this because his tools lie among the many bones of his victims.

We also know, very roughly, the dates of Zinj's brief life. By analyzing the minerals at Olduvai with an atomic testing device scientists have deduced that Zinj is almost two million years old. Even though that sounds incredibly long ago, very recent reports suggest that a similar species existed possibly fourteen million years ago.

The Leakeys and other scientists concluded that the ancient, small-brained toolmaker was certainly not a human being; nor was he an ape. He was a creature in transition, an ape man beginning to use hands and tools and weapons to establish a place for himself on a planet teeming with life. Zinj and his kind weighed a robust

Digging on the sun-baked plain is slow and painstaking work. The Leakeys carefully brush aside the sand with camel's-hair brushes and dental picks.

120 to 150 pounds and roamed their valley as its masters. They shared Olduvai with a related type of ape man who had the same size brain but was more delicately built, weighing only 40 to 90 pounds.

Traces of these two coexistent ape men have also been found in other parts of Africa. Some forty years ago the skull of a baby representing the smaller type was found by workmen in a chunk of rock blasted from a limestone quarry near the village of Taungs, South Africa. Raymond Dart, the anatomist at Johannesburg's University of Witwatersrand who studied the skull, realized the importance of the "Taungs baby" at once. But he had to wait more than twenty-five years before further studies and discoveries convinced his colleagues throughout the world.

Today we know that ape men in various forms survived over an enormous stretch of time. There is reason to believe that they existed from the era when they flourished in the Olduvai Gorge almost up to the twentieth century. Furthermore, they probably lived in much the same way throughout that period, going about in bands of ten to two hundred individuals, sleeping in trees or on rocky ledges, waking at sunrise, rarely wandering more than a few miles from their starting point, and returning to sleep again at sunset. Nor do we have evidence of any striking changes in their tools.

Yet evolution was on the move. Important changes of a more subtle sort were taking place. Whenever small, inbreeding groups live in isolation from other groups, new characteristics may suddenly appear, and traits that would be lost or buried in a vast population have a better chance to develop. This is what happened among the ape men; the result was a wide variety of physical types. Most of the types died out. But at least one of them developed particularly well in mind and body. He slowly forged forward in the struggle for survival.

This is the creature whom we regard as the earliest form of true man. He first appears about 400,000 years ago, give or take a few hundred centuries. We know him by his fossil remains, which have been found in Java, China, Germany, England, and the valley of the Jordan in Israel, as well as in Africa. The African finds have been along the coasts of Algeria and Morocco, in the Transvaal of South Africa, and also at Olduvai—but in a geologic layer laid down long after Zinj's lava plain was covered over.

Early man differed from his predecessors in many ways. For example, although he weighed about the same as Zinj,

Above is the 25,000,000-year-old fossil of a caterpillar. Fossils are either the preserved remains of creatures or imprints made in mud that has since become stone.

he was taller (five feet or so, compared with Zinj's four to four and a half feet). Also, the structure of his pelvis and other bones indicates that he could walk more efficiently. But by far the most significant difference was the size of his cranium. His brain was about twice as large as that of the average ape man. Even more important than the increase itself is the fact that it came about in a relatively short time—perhaps within 200,000 years, which is extremely fast for such a marked evolutionary change.

There was a high premium big brains for a very special reason. In a sense, man was beginning to lift himself by his own bootstraps. To a greater extent than any previously existing species, early Stone Age people sought to improve their way of life by using their heads: they invented hunting methods and developed a hunting psychology. Whereas Zinj had concentrated on getting his meat by killing rodents and lizards and other small creatures, or from the immature offspring of large animals, early man was more ambitious. He went after big game as well as small fry, probably driving large animals into swampy places where they were bogged down and could neither fight back effectively nor run away.

This hunting method called for more than rugged individualism. It demanded cooperation, planning, and the design of strategies based on some knowledge of the habits of potential victims. To succeed as a hunter of big game, man needed a larger and more effective brain. Self-control was absolutely necessary during the planning and cornering stages. Even when the animal had been slaughtered, man could not give free rein to his urge to gorge on red meat. The food had to be shared with women and children, and with older, experienced men who could no longer hunt.

New tools were developed for the hunt. Along with the choppers and bashers of the ape men we find picklike implements, spheroids, many-faceted stones perhaps hurled as missiles, and specially-sharpened chips or flakes used for cutting. The most characteristic weapon of all was the hand axe, a roughly pear-shaped tool generally rounded at one end and pointed at the other. The hand axe, which with the passing of time tended to become more common and more beautifully worked, served as a multipurpose tool for cutting, punching, chopping, and digging. Among other artifacts of the first men are the earliest-known hearths. These men were the first creatures to tame fire; they probably used it first for heat and later for cooking.

Other indirect clues suggest that they had some form

TEXT CONTINUED ON PAGE 49

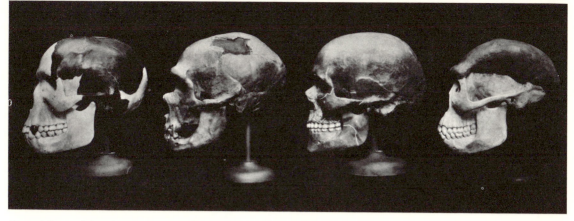

From left to right above are attempted restorations of the skulls of four early men: Piltdown (later proved unauthentic), Neanderthal, Cro-Magnon (Upper Paleolithic), and Java. Missing parts of each skull have been filled in.

Below is a front view of the skull of the Java man and a reconstruction of his head. A reconstruction such as this is put together by a specialized team of sculptor-anthropologists working to achieve an accurate interpretation.

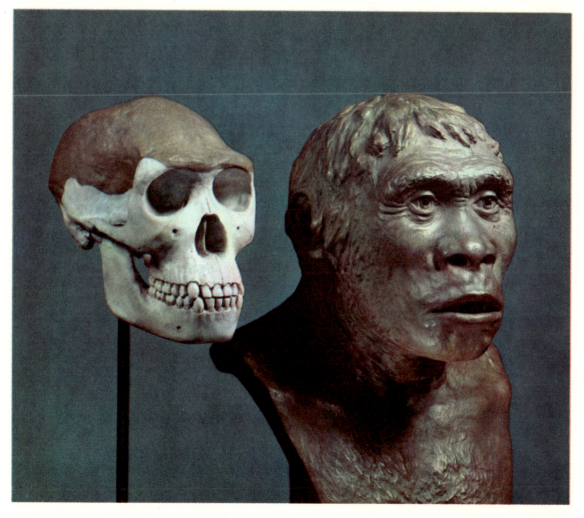

43

AN UPRIGHT MAN-APE

The first creature to stand upright and use tools probably lived three or four million years ago during the Pliocene epoch. Remains of this manlike primate have not yet been found, but his skull may have resembled a modern ape's (left). Note the small brain cavity, high brow-ridge, and the flat nose and large jaw. The manlike primate used his hands for fighting,

AN APE MAN WHO HUNTED

Zinj belonged to a group of South African ape men called *Australopithecus*. They lived during the Lower Paleolithic period as early as two million years ago. The brain of this ape man was slightly larger than that of the ape, but his jawbone was smaller. He held his head erect, and possibly he had the power of speech. His tools were pebbles (the front and back

A MAN WHO COULD COOK

About 360,000 years ago, in the second half of the Lower Paleolithic period, the first true man appeared. The skull and reconstruction shown here are those of Peking man, a fossilized skeleton found in a Chinese cave. His brain was twice as large as that of the ape, and his cranium was higher and more rounded. A typical tool was a crude chopper (at right)

A MAN WITH NEW WEAPONS

The first evidence of true man discovered in Europe was Steinheim man and his contemporary, Swanscombe man. They lived 250,000 years ago and were very much like men today, although their bones were thicker. The whole Steinheim skull was not found (the jaw was missing), but the brain size can be estimated from the cranium, which is little larger

A MAN WHO MADE BETTER TOOLS

Neanderthal man is not considered our direct ancestor; he had special characteristics not found in modern man. His physique was adjusted to the severe climate of the glacial period. He had a big head with a correspondingly large brain, face, and nose. He was heavy and muscular but stood only 5 feet 4 inches tall. The earlier Neanderthals of 90,000 years

A MAN WHO COULD PAINT

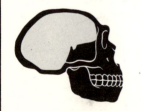

Upper Paleolithic man followed the Neanderthals into Europe. The newcomer lived from 30,000 to 10,000 years ago. He was almost like us; slightly shorter but with a lean and slender body. His skull and brain were of moderate size, and his facial features were no different from ours. He was quite a talented artist and craftsman who was capable of ab-

picking fruit, and hurling rocks. Perhaps his best tool was a heavy branch-club, right. At far right is a painting by Maurice Wilson of one such prehistoric and nearly human creature.

Branch Club

sides of two are at right) which he used to kill and skin small animals. Some ape men were less than 5 feet tall; others weighed up to 150 pounds and stood as tall as full-sized men.

Pebble Tools

that was well suited for working hides. There is evidence that Peking man could preserve and use fire. He soon learned how to cook meat and keep his family warm in the winter months.

Crude Chopping Tool

than Peking man's. At far right is a reconstruction of the head of Steinheim man. He had the sense to construct a good hand axe and other weapons for hunting large animals.

Fine Hand Axe

ago used the large Mousterian scraper (left tool) and saw-tooth points (right) to chop up their bear meat and other food. Neanderthal man disappeared about 40,000 years ago.

Scraper   *Saw-tooth Tools*

stract conception. Among his specialized tools was a flint with one razor-like edge and one blunted edge (right). This ingenious tool, known as a backed blade, evolved into the modern knife.

Backed Blade   *Knife*

46

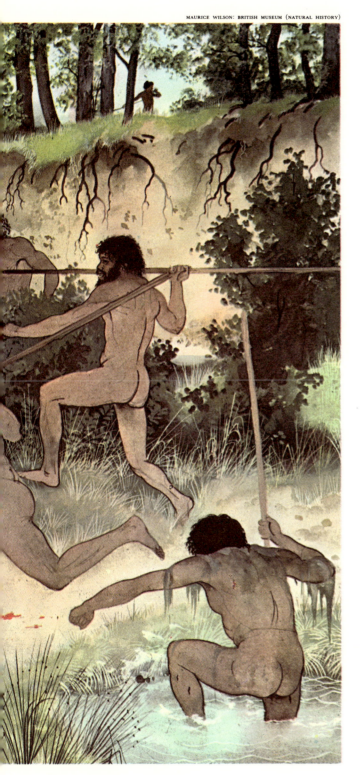

Swanscombe man lived in England 250,000 years ago. As one of the earliest-known true men, he and his kind developed techniques that enabled them to hunt big-game animals such as deer (left). The method of hunting had changed considerably from that of Zinj, who ate only coarse vegetation and snakes, rodents, and other small animals he could easily kill with a stone.

PILTDOWN FAKE

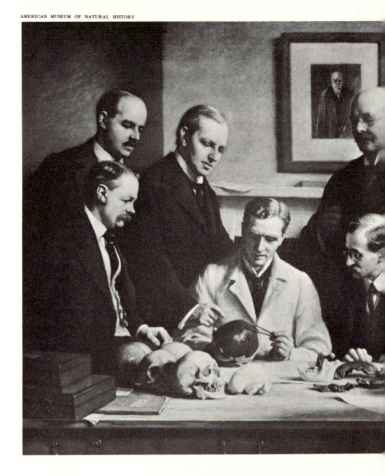

The skull of a large-brained ape man was discovered in 1912 by amateur archaeologist Charles Dawson in a gravel deposit near Piltdown Common, England. It was presumed to be the remains of "the most ancient-known inhabitant of England, if not of Europe." The discovery aroused extreme interest among scientists, and in the following year caused a controversy when two anthropologists attempted to reconstruct the shape of the head. Below are sketches representing their conflicting guesses: at left is a creature half man and half ape; the drawing at right shows a modern-looking man. Not until 1953 was it proved conclusively that the skull was a fake. It was a modern human skull cleverly attached to the jaw of an ape; Dawson himself may have been responsible for the hoax. In the painting at right, scientists compare various skulls with the Piltdown. At far right below is the New York Times *report of the result.*

BOTH: *Illustrated London News*

of language. The trick of making a very simple tool, say, a pebble chopper, can be learned by observing and imitating and perhaps by receiving a grunt of encouragement now and then. But shaping a hand axe is something else again. It involves sculpturing of a sort, the idea of a form quite different from that of the original stone, some delicate flaking—and, in all likelihood, words to convey all this to apprentices. Moreover, it seems unlikely that increasingly clever hunting tactics could have been worked out without the development of verbal communications.

There is also some more specific evidence of what happened next to this advanced axemaker. In a gravel pit at Swanscombe in Kent, England, on a high terrace of the Thames River, English scientists found the back half of a skull. According to Kenneth Oakley of the British Museum of Natural History, the skull is "indistinguishable from the corresponding parts of some skulls of modern man, although exceptionally thick." Another skull discovered in another gravel pit at Steinheim in southern Germany is also surprisingly modern in many respects. These two specimens are about 250,000 years old, and the general consensus is that they represent a stage between earliest man and our own species, modern man.

In describing these changes, we have come a long way from the Olduvai ape men toward the twentieth century. Indeed, nearly 90 per cent of our journey back through time has been completed. At this stage man is already in the process of developing along entirely new lines, of transforming himself and his world. All other species besides man have evolved by means of mutations—random and as yet uncontrollable changes in the structure of complex molecules built into the nuclei of the body's cells.

Earliest man and the later men found at Swanscombe and Steinheim were also products of accidents, selected mutations. But at the same time men were evolving in another unique way. They were changing not only because of their inherited chemistry but also because of what they learned and what they wanted. They were establishing traditions and higher orders of social organization. The human brain, originally a result of random forces, began to be used to invent and to fulfill purposes and desires. In turn it was being shaped by those purposes and desires. A new process called cultural evolution was beginning.

And it is cultural evolution that gave energy to the later events we will watch taking place in the lovely and fortunate Valley of Caves.

NEANDERTHALS

IN THE VALLEY

Who or what was the first manlike creature to amble into Europe? We may never identify him beyond doubt; we may always have to state flatly that at one of the rock shelters in the Valley of Caves above the Vézère River there are some extremely ancient remains that date back 200,000 years. We can only assume that these are the remains of men something like the fully developed creatures found at Swanscombe and Steinheim—men who had come far in time and evolution from the African ape men.

But we have considerably more information on the two major waves of migration that came to the Valley of Caves in more recent prehistoric times.

The first of these people, Neanderthal men, appeared on earth about 90,000 years before the present era. The Neanderthals flourished, reproducing themselves for some two thousand generations (about 50,000 years), and then vanished.

They were followed by a second wave of people who came later in the Paleolithic era. Traces of these Upper Paleolithic people near les Eyzies date back 30,000 years —which makes them modern indeed compared to the Neanderthals and to the first men on earth.

During most of the Neanderthals' 50,000-year stay in Europe, they lived hard lives, coping with harsh glacial climates to the best of their abilities. Traces of these people are found at many sites along the banks of the Dordogne and Vézère rivers, not only in rock shelters in the little valley of Castel Merle and in the les Eyzies cliffs but also in caves and grottoes scattered throughout the area. The Neanderthal men knew this countryside well. It was their land for a period many times longer than the span of recorded time.

Today man meets the Neanderthals everywhere; archaeologists, amateur and professional, are by no means the only ones to discover their artifacts. Boys ready for

Neanderthal man had to be sufficiently agile and clever to hunt the huge animals of his times. One of these was the broad-antlered Irish elk (left).

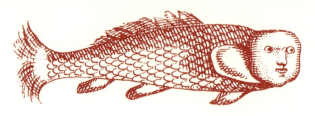

MEN, BEASTS, AND ANGELS

*Throughout the ages, artists and philosophers have specu-
lated freely about early man and his relationship to all
other animals. Collected here are some of the guesses made
before 1859 when the great British naturalist Charles
Darwin advanced his theory that men and apes evolved from
a common ancestor. In 1558, the map maker Guillaume Le
Testu showed even more imagination than other artists
of his day when he decorated a map with the two figures
at right; one has a dog's head, the other is without a head
but has a face on his chest. The eighteenth century saw
a blossoming of anthropological thought: at top is a man-
faced fish sketched by French naturalist J. B. Robinet;
above is a drawing by Georges de Buffon which depicts an
angel whispering to Nature that man is master over the
animals; at left is a study by the Swiss writer Johann
Lavater showing that faces of men and bulls are alike.*

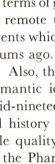

another adventure like that of the discovery of the Lascaux cave take long walks into the back country and often return with flints that human hands have chipped. A road-construction gang cuts into a hillside and finds a buried cave containing tools and skulls. Power-company workers putting up new electric lines pick Neanderthal artifacts out of the post holes.

But chances are that you will not hear much about the Neanderthals during a brief trip to les Eyzies. Tourists hardly ever visit the excavated sites because, aside from the scenery along the way, there is nothing much to see. For, as far as we know, the Neanderthals produced no cave paintings or engravings.

It has become almost a tradition to underrate these early settlers. The tradition started more than a century ago when the first discovery of the remains of a Neanderthal man was made in a narrow valley near Düsseldorf, Germany. Quarry workers had already done a thorough job of demolishing most of the valley's numerous caves, and the last two were being destroyed when the men noticed parts of a fossilized skeleton. The bones looked like those of a cave bear. But the remains turned out to be the skeleton of a man, a small and solidly built individual having massive brow ridges and thighbones and a heavy flattish skull.

That was in 1856, and since then attitudes have changed considerably. At that time scientists had a hazy view of the prehistoric past—particularly when it came to the origins of human beings. People did not think of prehistory in terms of geologic eras. They still had a tendency to think of remote times in terms of Noah's Ark and the Flood, events which had taken place no more than a few millenniums ago.

Also, there were many religious beliefs and some wholly romantic ideas which made it difficult for people of the mid-nineteenth century to view early man scientifically: all history had to have a kind of special glow, a fairy-tale quality. The Victorians were dazzled by the power of the Pharaohs, the glory of the Golden Age of Greece, the pageantry of flowering knighthood and chivalry in medieval times. Somehow the world of living citizens appeared less noble to them than the world of our historic ancestors, the princes and kings, heroes and prophets of times past.

Imagine how news of the 1856 discovery of Neanderthal man affected people imbued with these ideas. It was a case of injured vanity, a real skeleton in the closet. A

TEXT CONTINUED ON PAGE 56

53

Early in the seventeenth century Jan Bruegel the Elder painted this lush vision of prehistory. Based on the Bible, it showed all of creation as the Garden of Eden with Adam and Eve (under the tree, above) surrounded by

perfectly paired animals. In Genesis, God decreed that man, the highest of His creations, should "have dominion over the fish of the sea, and over the fowl of the air, and over every living thing that moveth upon the earth."

proud aristocratic family confronted in public with evidence of an unsavory relative could not have reacted more violently. There was revulsion and shocked disbelief. A myth was manufactured that these bones could not possibly have belonged to an ancestor but might be the remains of some strange and deformed creature.

Everything on the plus side was ignored—such as the fact that the Neanderthal skull had enclosed a large brain, at least as large as most modern brains. One English scientist expressed his distaste in particularly vivid terms: "It may have been one of those wild men, half-crazed, half-idiotic, cruel and strong, who are always more or less to be found living on the outskirts of barbarous tribes and who now and then appear in civilized communities to be consigned perhaps to the penitentiary or the gallows when their murderous propensities manifest themselves."

Other specialists disagreed with the idea that the bones belonged to a demented savage. They said variously that the man had been a diseased hermit, an old Dutchman, an ancient Celt, a Cossack killed while helping to drive Napoleon's army out of Russia in 1812.

Of course, no one today seriously believes that the Neanderthal skull was that of an alien or a freak who lived only a few centuries ago. Later finds, some of the most important having been made not far from les Eyzies, amply confirm the statements of the few scientists who in 1856 were convinced that this specimen belonged to a prehistoric era. But the old prejudices would not die. Even today some text and reference books accept theories that reflect and perpetuate the Victorian feeling of revulsion, claiming that even though Neanderthal man represents a true prehistoric ancestor, he was certainly apelike and brutish.

This claim is based mainly on the study of the original Neanderthal skeleton, which turned out to be that of an old man suffering from such a serious case of arthritis that his spine, his jaw, and possibly his limbs had been affected. Then several years ago two anatomists wrote what should be the last word on the actual appearance of Neanderthal man. A number of fossil skeletons had been found in France and moved to the Musée de l'Homme in Paris. In them the anatomists found nothing to support the notion that Neanderthal man shuffled along flat-footed with head thrust forward and knees bent or that he was coarsely built and generally uncouth.

The anatomists summarized their conclusions as follows: "There is thus no valid reason for the assumption

A group of distinguished French archaeologists are pictured (right) at the cave of la Mouthe in 1902. This excursion was one part of a conference which officially recognized the existence of prehistoric cave art. Below, men pry rocks out of a crude and amateurish excavation at Laugerie Basse in 1908.

Three Neanderthal men fight a cave bear for possession of a rock shelter in this C. R. Knight painting.

that the posture of Neanderthal man . . . differed significantly from that of present-day men . . . If he could be reincarnated and placed in a New York subway—provided that he were bathed, shaved, and dressed in modern clothing—it is doubtful whether he would attract any more attention than some of its other denizens." To be sure, this statement has a certain ambiguity. It is not altogether clear whether the authors were saying that some subway riders look a bit on the primitive side or whether they were paying Neanderthal man a full-fledged compliment.

New facts about Neanderthal man began to emerge with discoveries made during the years following the first controversial find in Germany, particularly with a series of excavations carried out along the Dordogne and Vézère rivers shortly before World War I. Here were found fossilized remains just like the original skeleton, and to these the term Neanderthal was also applied. Of the several Neanderthal sites in the Valley of Caves, one of the most important is located a mere five miles from les Eyzies on the road to Castel Merle and Lascaux. It is le Moustier, a site so important that the French call Neanderthals Mousterian men.

Not far from the road in the village of le Moustier is an area surrounded by a high wire fence to discourage amateur prehistorians. This is the site of a limestone cave most of which has long since crumbled away, but which provided prehistoric people with adequate living quarters for thousands of years. The cave was discovered in 1856, when the only way you could reach the village was by coach and on horseback. It has been excavated extensively since then, but inside the fence under an overhanging part of the ancient cave is a many-layered section of untouched earth. The earth is full of flints. You can see any number of them, in place, along the neatly cut edges of the section, and no one knows what further evidence lies buried inside. The section is being kept intact, partly as an open-air museum and partly for the benefit of future scientists who will dig here with improved techniques.

Many things have been discovered in le Moustier. One finding has special significance, however, in the light it sheds on the true nature of Neanderthal man. Late one winter evening in 1908, a Swiss-German investigator who was excavating the site rushed to the spot at the urging of an excited assistant. Human remains had been found in a deep layer, and that is a major event in any investigation of prehistory. But there was more to it than that. Excavation revealed the almost complete skeleton of a boy about fifteen

TEXT CONTINUED ON PAGE 62

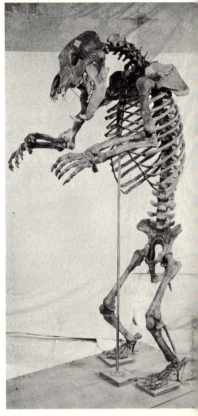

From this eight-foot skeleton of a cave bear it is easy to imagine what the live animal looked like. The exact appearance of Neanderthal man is harder to visualize.

59

JOHN HUEHNERGARTH

CHARLES R. KNIGHT: AMERICAN MUSEUM OF NATURAL HISTORY

A Neanderthal family is alarmed by a herd
of Pleistocene mammoths in the painting
below by C. R. Knight. The artist has por-
trayed three family prototypes: the mother;
the industrious flint-making grandfather;
the alert and dauntless hunter. At left
is a cartoon that shows the same charac-
ters in modern clothes. It supports the
recent theory that the cave men would not
look out of place if they were moved from
their shelter into the New York subway.

A Neanderthal grave was uncovered at the excavation of Combe Grenal in the Dordogne Valley. No bones were in the pit (left)—less than a hundred prehistoric human remains have ever been discovered. The arrangement of large stones and slabs on top of the pit is reconstructed in the cross-section view at right.

TEXT CONTINUED FROM PAGE 59

or sixteen years old, and the position of the skeleton suggested a most intriguing possibility.

The boy had not been tossed haphazardly into some corner of the cave. According to official reports on the find, he had been placed on his side in a trench in a sleeping position, knees slightly drawn up and head resting on his right forearm. A pile of flints lay under his head, forming a sort of stone pillow. Furthermore, it seems that his people believed in some kind of afterlife, for flint tools were buried with the boy, including a beautifully worked hand axe placed near his hand. Also, there were indications of what might have been an offering of roasted meat. Located around the boy's remains were wild-cattle bones, many of them charred.

As the various parts of this scene fit into place, it acquires enormous importance, particularly when considered against the background of records dating back to the more remote past. As far as we know, neither the ape man of Africa nor representatives of earliest man in Europe ever bothered to bury their dead. They died like all other animals, dropping in their tracks or wandering off alone to wait for the end. The first evidence of burials and associated rituals comes from Neanderthal times, and the report on the le Moustier boy is only one of those which point to the

The first Neanderthal site to become known in France was the cave at le Moustier, seen below in a 1908 photograph. As shown in the painting on the preceding pages, the cave was originally more commodious and overlooked the river.

prehistoric practice of superstitious and religious rites.

Signs of such burials exist at other sites in the Valley of Caves and also far from France. The search for Neanderthal man's traces leads us through wild and isolated parts of the world—for example, along footpaths at the edges of precipices and down ravines gashed high into the side of a mountain in the republic of Uzbek in Central Asia. In one of the ravines there is a cave called Teshik-Tash, "the rock with the hole in it," where a Soviet scientist, led by children from a nearby village, found the skull of a young boy in a shallow grave. Arranged around the head end of the grave and stuck point-down into the ground were half a dozen pairs of curved horns, the horns of the Siberian ibex, or wild goat. Perhaps, the scientist concluded, the practice of ibex worship, which still goes on in Central Asia, had its origins among the Neanderthals.

Even more has been learned about the Neanderthals' rituals, which involved the most widely hunted animal of their times, the cave bear. On another mountain, this one located in eastern Austria, is a cave known as the Dragon's Lair; here Neanderthal people built a rectangular vault with a thick limestone slab serving as the lid. For religious reasons that we cannot apprehend, they put seven complete cave-bear skulls inside the vault, all facing in the direction of the cave's entrance.

At other sites it was the custom to pile the bear skulls one on top of the other in symmetrical pyramids or to set them on long poles driven into the ground. Sometimes the bones of the giant animals were arranged in special positions. The most recent discovery of a place where Neanderthal people organized a cave-bear cult takes us back to the les Eyzies neighborhood again, to a site near Lascaux which was excavated in 1961 and includes a human skeleton. On the ground around the skeleton were laid the bones of more than twenty bears.

Investigators are constantly on the lookout for patterns like this. Bones and rocks placed in orderly ways are like the symbols of a strange language yet to be deciphered. But what do the symbols mean? If we could interpret them as we do Egyptian hieroglyphics or medieval manuscripts we might feel closer to those prehistoric men and women.

Neanderthal hunters drive ibexes over the edge of a gorge in the Caucasus Mountains while other men wait below to kill the stunned animals. This scene was recreated by Zdenek Burian from prehistoric finds made in Russia.

And we might even grasp then the ideas and emotions behind their activities. No mere brute could have been so concerned about the meaning of death and the passing of a loved one, nor could he have imagined an afterlife and thereby taken the first faltering steps toward conceiving a religion.

Neanderthal man was also fairly clever. In the parts of Europe where we have observed him, he contended successfully with conditions that became more and more demanding. Appearing on the scene during a period of glacial retreat, he found a warm, temperate climate and reasonably easy living. Then the nature of his world became more challenging. The glaciers started advancing again, as they had twice before during the Ice Age. Seas of ice crept southward into Europe from Scandinavian lands and northward from the mountains of the Alps and the Pyrenees, and Neanderthal man was partially trapped in a glacial pincer-movement.

He gradually adapted to the climate change in two ways: physically and through his own inventions. His body began to develop differently; he became smaller and stockier. The son of hardy parents fared better. If he inherited certain characteristics (such as body hair) that favored existence in cold weather, he lived longer than his contemporaries. And in living longer, he produced more children.

But cultural adaptation was equally important. As far as Neanderthal man was concerned, the Ice Age was the era when he began to make creative use of fire. He had used fire ages before, but now he used it more resourcefully and more extensively. He may even have found how to make it. If so, the discovery was probably accidental, occurring when he was striking stones together to shape tools. If he did not learn to be a fire maker, it is difficult to explain how he had fire at his command throughout a period when fires produced by volcanoes and other natural phenomena were no more common than they are now.

Neanderthal man used fire for a number of purposes besides warming himself and his food. Caves were refuges where the families had to seek shelter during severe winters, and torches must have been wielded to drive bears and other animal cave dwellers out. Also, hunters probably put their wooden spearheads in the fire to char them, making fire-hardened tips.

The widespread use of fire may have produced another interesting result. For men without fire, as for apes and

The Greeks explained man's possession of fire with the myth that Prometheus had stolen it from heaven.

Neanderthals are thought to have been the first fire makers. Peking man (above) could use a blaze when he found it but had no tools to make fire.

ape men, the day ended with the setting of the sun; night was a time to huddle together, to sleep the vigilant sleep of animals that must be ready to wake swiftly in order to flee or to fight. But with fire, man learned to do more than merely keep his enemies away. Fire lengthened his day and gave him a few more hours to work and plan and relax.

Some of the routines of the Neanderthals' day-to-day lives may be deduced from sites in the valley and elsewhere. If you were an observer at one of their rock shelters, you would hear voices speaking a language which had advanced far beyond the guttural-grunt stage. Inside the shelter women would be seen involved in a number of chores. One of the older women is scraping off the inner side of an animal pelt. When cleaned, the hide is to be used for clothing or as a blanket or, set upon poles, as a windbreak to protect sleepers from icy blasts. Another woman throws wood on the precious fire and calls to some of the older children. They will soon go out to gather more wood, as well as fruits and tender parts of plants to be used for the day's meal or to store away as part of an emergency food supply. They may also gather medicinal herbs and leaves to dress wounds and to relieve some of the symptoms of disease.

There is a workshop area out in front of the shelter. A skilled toolmaker sits on a stone or log, hard at his job, and you would have to watch a long while and make many mistakes and ask many questions before you could begin to master his simplest techniques. He takes a hard piece, or nodule, of flint shaped something like a discus, and working with another stone as a hammer, bangs the nodule around the edges. Gradually he succeeds in knocking off small flakes all around the rim. He trims one face of the nodule by striking off more flakes and then prepares for the next crucial step. He sets the nodule end up, and with a sharp, well-directed blow on the edge, detaches a large flat flake. This flake's outer surface is the pretrimmed face. Some finer trimming of the flake produces a flint point which may serve as a spearhead or as a hand-wielded pick.

Such a tool is the result of an exactly conceived plan. Fixed in the mind of the maker was an image of what he was working toward. The Neanderthals knew how to make many tools—theirs was the most varied tool kit yet developed by man. And for each tool there was an exact concept among a given group. In addition to weapons, they made different kinds of scrapers, drills, knives, planers, and an assortment of other implements. They also made

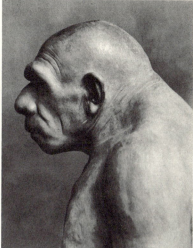

Artists and anthropologists are still trying to paint an accurate picture of Neanderthal man. Below is a full figure by Maurice Wilson, who made several anthropological drawings for this book. At right are two sculptured attempts: the first is pug-nosed, the second is stoop-shouldered.

some hand axes, the same kind of tool that the world's first men had made so long ago; after nearly 300,000 years of development, these axes were still useful to Neanderthal man under certain circumstances. Man's mechanical skill was advancing slowly.

Equipped with his tools, Neanderthal man became a master at hunting big game. Like earlier man he probably preferred going after the young animals that were easiest to snare. But he also killed his share of older, battle-wise veterans. According to studies made at the Dragon's Lair site in Austria, bears may have been smoked out of their caves and driven through narrow passages between large boulders where they could be attacked from above with spears and clubs and stone missiles. It was a dangerous business, but estimates based on bone count indicate that some ten thousand cave bears were killed at this site alone.

In other Neanderthal locations, herds of wild goats appear to have been chased toward steep, narrow ravines. Some of the animals jumped across to safety, but others lost their footing in the scramble or were too young to make the leap successfully. And when they fell, men were ready at the bottoms of the ravines.

The hunters did not always rely on traps provided by the natural layout of the land. They must have made traps of their own to kill giants like the woolly rhinoceroses and mammoths. The feat almost certainly required camouflaged pitfalls such as those constructed by hunting tribes still living today.

Our picture of Neanderthal man is based on scenes such as these, scenes which have been reconstructed from excavated pieces of rock and bone. And the picture seems quite vivid, considering the scantiness of the evidence. We have indeed learned a great deal about Neanderthal man, but many major questions are unanswered. Satisfactory answers can only be given after much more study. One of the most intensive areas of study is the Valley of Caves, where a brilliant prehistorian has been unearthing much new information. His reports suggest many things—the most striking of which is how much there is still to learn.

Some Neanderthal groups perished as glaciers advanced into Europe (left); others were absorbed by more advanced tribes. Above is a heavy flint hand axe, one of the tools which remain as clues to the cave men's existence.

71

IV

MYSTERY AT COMBE GRENAL

The little side valley of Combe Grenal is hard to find; once you have succeeded, it is even more difficult to discover the extraordinary Neanderthal site that is located there. To reach it from les Eyzies you take a road that runs past two of the most famous painted caves—done by Upper Paleolithic people who came after the Neanderthals. You drive through the medieval town of Sarlat and on across the Dordogne River. By this time you are on a narrow macadam road heading for Domme, a charming village surrounded by an ancient wall and set on a high cliff overlooking the Dordogne Valley.

Before getting to Domme, you turn off to a still narrower dirt road that runs along the river at the foot of the cliff, and then off again to a very bumpy uphill road partly overgrown with grass. This is the road that passes through the Combe Grenal Valley, but now the problem is knowing when to stop. The only clue to the site's location is two or three cars parked half in the bushes and half on the road, and even then the search is not over.

You still have to find the half-hidden path that winds up a wooded slope. The path leads to a small terrace— from there the site can be seen as a hollowed-out mass of limestone, weathered gray and yellow-gold and pink, and outlined sharply against the green slope of the hill. There are shadows at the back of the rock in the hollow places; these are grottoes that do not extend far into the hillside. They are all that remain of what was a high and spacious cave. The vaulted ceiling has collapsed, but the past has left extremely important traces here.

The man in charge of the Combe Grenal site, as well as of archaeological investigations in the entire les Eyzies

At the Combe Grenal shelter (left), archaeologists are finding traces of the Neanderthal groups who lived there intermittently for 50,000 years.

Aristotle (384–322 B.C.)

Carolus Linnaeus (1707–1778)

Charles Darwin (1809–1882)

region, is François Bordes, professor of prehistory at the University of Bordeaux. He ranks as one of the world's leading authorities on Neanderthal man. A thorough and astute investigator and a first-rate teacher, he works with his wife, Denise de Sonneville-Bordes, who is a professional prehistorian in her own right.

Born in a village not far from les Eyzies, François Bordes became intrigued with prehistory at an early age. When he was ten years old he read an exciting science-fiction novel about cave men. Four years later he did his first excavating in a valley about eighteen miles from his home. After he began finding traces of prehistoric people, he was often seen bicycling to and from the site with heavy bundles of flint tools on his back. Eventually he took a degree in geology but shifted from science to sabotage during World War II.

He joined the French Resistance forces, an experience he recalls with some relish: "It was the first time in my life that I could do things like blowing up railroad tracks and not get punished for it." He would certainly have received the maximum punishment, however, if the Nazis had caught him, for he was on their death list. After the war and an administrative interlude in Paris at the National Center of Scientific Research, Bordes returned to the south of France to pursue prehistory on a full-time basis. The Combe Grenal site represents his most intensive project to date; he has been working there since 1953.

We cannot tell exactly when the first Neanderthal man came across this spot in his search for a home. It may have been ninety thousand or a hundred thousand years ago, during a period of warm preglacial climate. He was probably wary about entering the shelter: unfriendly hunters, or even more unfriendly lions or cave bears, might already have found the site to their liking. After an inspection tour in which he found that the cave was unoccupied, he returned to his group with the good news. Up the slope they came to move in, perhaps thirty to fifty people in the entire company.

The group stayed for a long time. Many fires burned and sputtered out here, leaving ashes and charred bits of wood. Many pieces of flint were carried to the cave from a quarry higher up in the woods on the hill; many chips and flakes and discarded flint tools were scattered on the earth floor during the course of daily living. The people and their children and their children's children brought in branches and twigs to burn, plants and roots to eat, grasses for beds, pelts and bones, and various other things. All this material decayed and crumbled away and accumulated. Pressed down by human feet and by its own weight, it formed a many-layered carpet, or living floor.

No one knows how long the original Neanderthal group or its descendants remained at Combe Grenal; there is no proven relationship between the thickness of a layer in the living floor and the duration of an occupation. Nor do we know why they left. They may have died off in an epidemic or been annihilated by another group, or they may have left on their own because game animals had become scarce.

In any case, they did leave after several generations.

Professor François Bordes points to one of the earth layers at the Combe Grenal site. By analyzing the many levels, Bordes seeks to understand the patterns of prehistoric life. His specialized work is made possible by many famous and more general scientists who preceded him: Aristotle, the first biologist; Linnaeus, the botanist who classified plants and animals; and Darwin, the first evolutionist.

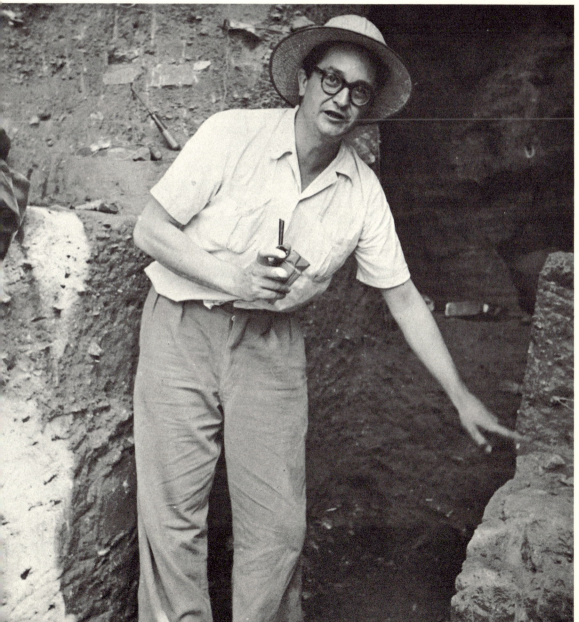

In this diagram of the excavation, the cave itself is seen at rear, and the layers are clearly exposed—some laden with flints. Black lines in the photograph (right) are hearth layers containing ashes, charcoal, and bones.

And for centuries unheard winds blew into and around a place where human beings had been, covering the living floor with dust and sand. Rain-swollen streams added rubble and silt as a new layer of earth formed and further compressed the remains beneath it. This was a sterile layer, the mark of a site deserted—but it was not deserted for good.

The original searcher had chosen well. Neanderthal people came to Combe Grenal again and again over a period of fifty thousand years or so. During more recent times other people came—the cave painters. And most recently of all, the prehistorians arrived. François Bordes and his colleagues have now removed many tons of dirt and boulders from the site. They have dug from the top through some thirty feet of deposits down to bedrock and the original living floor. Working very carefully, and keeping sharp eyes out for subtle changes in the color and consistency of different soils, they have identified more than fifty distinct layers and sublayers.

Care and vigilance pay off in excavations. About half-way down in the deposit, Bordes noted a circular patch of fine dark soil standing out in an ashy layer. He removed only this peculiar soil, not touching the surrounding material, and ended up with a hole about eight inches deep. A plaster cast of the hole showed that a wooden shaft had been driven into the ground. He concluded that perhaps it was one of a row of shafts used to support skins or woven branches which formed a barrier at the mouth of the cave. There was also a small grave about twenty-five feet down,

A view of the front of the excavation (right) shows that stone walls have been built to protect exposed earth layers from winter storms. At left two young assistants dig into the topmost layer of the shelter; in back of them are senior archaeologists.

not far from the level of the original Combe Grenal settlers; it was probably the grave of a child.

These findings cònfirm evidence about Neanderthal man's living habits that has been obtained at other sites. But Combe Grenal has yielded far more than that. It has given us an entirely new way of thinking about Neanderthal culture. The findings have indicated that the most important thing is not the materials themselves but the knowledge that may be derived from the careful analysis of tools.

During nine summers of painfully slow digging, more than 75,000 pieces of flint have been found in Combe Grenal deposits. Bordes has examined all the pieces. Some 14,000 of these are tools, and he has recorded the position of every one of them, layer by layer. Furthermore, he has calculated the ratio of one kind of tool to another in each layer, and this is the crucial part of his method. He refuses to draw any sweeping conclusions about the entire Neanderthal culture: perhaps they were a highly varied group of tribes with no real relationship to each other. He insists on letting the stone pieces speak for themselves. Such a

At Combe Grenal the diggers found a vertical variation in the layers (*cross section above*) which suggested that a stake had been driven into the ground. A plaster cast of the hole was made (*right*); it strongly resembled a stake. Below is a sketch of what may have happened: Neanderthal men set up posts at the entrance of their shelter to give additional protection.

ruthlessly scientific attitude demands time, and it also demands attention to an enormous amount of detail. But unless this method is used, there will be no significant advances in our knowledge of early man. Otherwise we will merely repeat the mistakes of the past, jumping from one prejudice to another.

What Bordes ends up with after an intensive period of work is not, therefore, a neat story that ties together a series of deductions—not that, but a batch of equally revealing statistics. For example, take his careful examination of the fourteenth layer of the Combe Grenal living floor. Nearly half of the 766 tools found there belong to a single general category. This category consists of flint flakes each of which has one edge with a number of curved notches (usually three or four) set close together to form a kind of ripple. There is also a large proportion of flakes with only one curved notch. It should be pointed out that this layer contains many other kinds of tools such as a few spear points, some flint blades and scrapers, and even a couple of hand axes.

But the layer's characteristic feature is the high proportion of notched tools. It happens that of the fifty-odd layers at Combe Grenal, nine others have almost identically the same proportion of notched tools to other tools. If every layer had radically different tool proportions, you could not hope to recognize meaningful patterns in the system, and you might give up trying to count the number of tools of which category were in which layer. But with as many as nine layers being similar, we can conclude that there are definite patterns here—statistical clues for those who are patient enough to look for them.

The site includes other patterns. In some layers up to three out of every four tools are scrapers of various kinds, and about 20 per cent of the scrapers are so similar that you could quickly learn to spot most of them. Some of these are thick, solid flakes with a special overlapping, or "fish-scale," effect along the edges. They are beautiful examples of prehistoric craftsmanship. In a few layers there is a high proportion of thin, flattish scrapers—but thick scrapers make up no more than one per cent of the total.

What can we hope to find out by analyzing the frequency with which these three types of tools occur? Specifically, what do the numbers of notched tools or thick or thin scrapers tell us about a world of human beings that no longer exists? Important things have already been learned, but the past is just beginning to reveal its secrets.

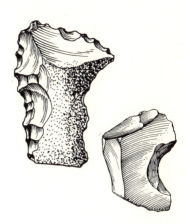

Here are three varieties of flint tools found in the layers. Above are two notched implements that may have been used for sawing; below is a thick scraping tool; at bottom is a thin scraper (Mousterian point) measuring about three inches high.

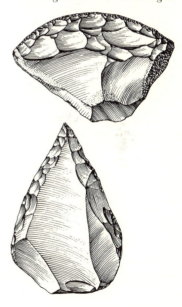

This woodcut of the Neanderthal Gorge, Germany, was made shortly before the famous skull was found there by quarry workers in 1856.

A major finding to date is that in a strict sense there is no such thing as Neanderthal man if that name implies a standardized sort of human being who lived in pretty much the same way wherever he settled. These were flesh-and-blood people whose lives were far more complicated and varied than has hitherto been suspected. A second finding is that Neanderthal man did not develop at an even rate, improving gradually with each advancing millennium. At Combe Grenal you find no evidence of cultural evolution as it is conventionally conceived. Tools are not crude at the bottom layers and increasingly refined farther toward the top.

Thirdly, we suspect that each type of layer with its characteristic tool kit represents a distinct way of life. One group would move in, presumably because hunting conditions were right, and then they would move out when circumstances changed. Later a similar group or a group with different traditions would reoccupy the site for their own reasons, and so on and on over the centuries. This conclusion seems possible because fully developed notched-tool layers lie above and below fully developed thick-scraper and thin-scraper layers, and there is no particular sequence.

Right now we know very little about the different cultures. Yet the notched-tool layers do imply the existence of a tribe that specialized in woodworking. The minute you see the rippled edge of a notched tool you are reminded of a crude but effective saw. Furthermore, the single-notched tools were probably used to scrape selected branches and smooth them into shafts for spears, presumably spears with fire-hardened wooden tips, because so few flint points are found in these layers.

So Bordes' scientific method is already yielding a few conclusions. But it also continues to turn up facts and data that are almost totally mysterious.

One such fact is that the bones of wild horses are the chief fossils to be found in a number of notched-tool layers. What could this mean? For one thing, the habits of the Neanderthal people who are represented by these layers would certainly have been influenced by the habits of the animals they hunted. And if they hunted horses, they would have had to become wanderers themselves. For the horse, unlike such game as the reindeer and the caribou, has sense enough to move out of a territory where it is being hunted. But the deduction that these people were nomadic seems to have no connection at all with the fact that they used notched tools.

Similarly we can only spin out the theories and guesses in attempting to account for thick-scraper layers. What were these people doing that required so many of these heavy scrapers? Since there is no evidence that the thick-scraper people hunted any particular animal in preference to another, they may have been using the tools to treat a variety of hides and pelts in a special way. Perhaps they had learned to make improved clothing by cleaning skins more thoroughly, a process that might call for heavy-duty scrapers. And what are we to make of the observation that most Neanderthal burials occur in these thick-scraper layers? Archaeology is full of such questions, which arouse wonder and cry for explanations.

Bordes is making a special effort to determine if any of his findings bear on the problem of where Neanderthal men came from and what happened to them ultimately. Some tools as old as 180,000 years have been found elsewhere, but none of that age have been unearthed at Combe Grenal. So the answer concerning origins may never come forth from these statistics. Yet there is a good chance that Bordes' layers may yield some conclusions regarding the Neanderthals' fate.

In the lower and middle layers, that is, from about 90,000 to 45,000 years ago, there are no significant and continued trends in the general quality of tools. But after that, specifically during the next five millenniums, changes begin to occur. We read a tragedy in the record—the

LE PRÉHISTORIEN DOIT PARFOIS FAIRE FACE À DES DIFFICULTÉS INCOMPRÉHENSIBLES

A French artist and prehistorian drew this cartoon of Neanderthals piling strange rocks in the way of diggers. Caption says: "The prehistorian must sometimes encounter incomprehensible difficulties."

decline and fall of a people who lived long before the Roman Empire and endured much longer.

Signs of this change appear in certain of the top layers which the horse hunters left. Their work becomes sloppier, and what their craftsmen make has the feel of cheap trinkets. Stone-shaping techniques are noticeably inferior to those used in lower layers. Flaking is less efficient, chips and broken-off pieces and other debris are far more common, and tools are proportionately fewer. Furthermore, the tools, even the standard weapons that have been made for thousands of generations, now have a cruder appearance and are less carefully made. The same sort of thing happens among upper thick-scraper layers and probably in thin-scraper layers as well.

At left Professor Bordes demonstrates how Neanderthal men made their tools. In his left hand he grasps a solid flint, or nodule. Then, working with a bone hammer in his right hand, he strikes the edge of the nodule, chipping it until it forms a point or a sharp edge. By this "knapping" process, Neanderthal men made such heavy-duty tools as scrapers and choppers. During the later stages of the Paleolithic era (which means "Old Stone Age") the process was considerably refined. In most parts of the world man used only stone tools up until the beginning of the Bronze Age 4,000 years ago.

Many theories have been devised to explain the decline. Perhaps it had something to do with the climate, or perhaps another, more advanced people were beginning to dominate the scene. Or perhaps, as some philosophers believe, cultures have a natural span of life and, like people, die when their time runs out. Bordes, the author of three fine science-fiction novels, and a man who certainly does not lack imagination, sums up the situation as follows: "I write science-fiction, but I don't use it in archaeology. We may yet learn what happened, but for that we will need more facts."

The picture has a somewhat brighter side, however. There is a fourth type of layer, a fourth identifiable Neanderthal settlement. Besides the people characterized by the notched tools and the flat and thin scrapers, this fourth tribe, if it can be called that, apparently evolved and progressed in striking ways. The people were highly inventive and made more varied kinds of tools than any of the other Neanderthal tribes. But what distinguishes their tool kit is that it contains great numbers of two kinds of tools: the hand axe and the backed blade, a flake sharpened at one edge and deliberately blunted at the other edge like the blade of a modern hunting knife.

During temperate preglacial times in Europe, these people used many hand axes. On the average, hand axes made up one fifth of their tools, and they also developed new forms of backed blades. A significant shift took place, however, when warm climates changed for the worse and the ice advanced again about 70,000 years ago. Hand axes dropped sharply to one fourth or less of their previous frequency, while the proportion of backed blades increased about five to ten times, from 2 to 3 per cent to as much as 20 per cent of all tools. If hand axes were often used to dig with, their decreasing popularity during cold periods may be connected with the fact that the ground was frozen solid much of the year. The increasing popularity of the backed blade implies a need for better woodworking equipment such as would be required to make traps, special shelters, extra-sharp poles and spears.

The main thing about these eminently practical and inventive people is that the backed blade and other tools they shaped were good enough to give ideas to the people who came after Neanderthal man. His tools comprised a kind of heritage for the ages, not as grand as the cave paintings, but a heritage nonetheless. In the tools we see that the Neanderthals did not merely adapt to harsh living

Prehistoric Man, AUGUSTA AND BURIAN: PUBLISHER—HAMLYN, LONDON AND ARTIA, PRAGUE

Above, a Neanderthal man attempts a difficult step in the art of the flintmaker: chipping away a flake from the nodule. This carefully wrought chip will perhaps be used for a spear point. Flint was a good stone for such purposes because it is hard (it will scratch most steels), and it will split just the way the toolmaker wants it to.

conditions and then disappear without a trace and without affecting subsequent prehistory. The sharp, solid, and well-worked flints these people left for other men to marvel at and copy are superb tools; but they are also more than tools. They are symbols of activities and ideas which were passed on to future generations.

So Neanderthal people, brutish subsavages to most of the Victorians, emerge in quite a different light today. Or rather they are beginning to emerge. Through the slowly dispersing mist that is our ignorance, we see them as human beings capable of fashioning beautiful tools and thinking about the nature of life and death. It is interesting to note that although no conclusive evidence has yet been found of any Neanderthal art, Bordes and other prehistorians are now convinced that some such art must have existed. Their argument is that it would be very surprising indeed if people who buried their dead and created rituals to appease imagined spirits had not also turned their minds to the creation of designs and images. Very often pieces of mineral paint (ocher for red and manganese dioxide for black) are found in Neanderthal layers.

High on a block of stone in front of the museum at les Eyzies, facing the valley from under a rock shelter, is a statue of a Neanderthal man that catches the quality of his abilities and his limitations. A massively built, monolithic figure looks out at the sky and the horizon. He seems to be reaching for something beyond his grasp, reaching as it were with his eyes and his brain. Yet he is somehow tied down. His hands, heavy and powerful, are held straight and stiff against his sides. This is the figure of an aspiring, yearning, groping individual—a human being who fell short of the people about to replace him. But he came very close.

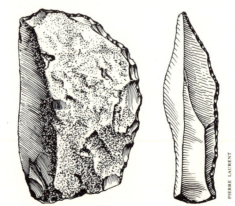

PIERRE LAURENT

The statue of Neanderthal man that stands above les Eyzies can be seen at the center of this photograph. Behind the statue is the cliff-hanging château which houses the les Eyzies Museum of Prehistory. At left are two examples of the Neanderthal backed blade, sharp edge turned to the right.

V

PHOTO BY ROMAIN ROBERT

THE CAVE ARTISTS

The Lascaux cave may indeed be prehistory's finest monument, but the preliminaries to a first visit seem designed to kill any feelings of awe and mystery. You wait in line at the ticket office, follow the guide to a steel door in the side of a hill, and then you are herded in a group through the door which clangs shut behind you. There are electric lights, air conditioning, concrete stairs, and another steel door. There are times when French authorities close the cave entirely for fear of a strange, funguslike growth that has appeared on the walls.

Yet the minute you are permitted to pass through the second door, you forget about the modern world. You enter into a high, vaulted, oval-shaped chamber covered with painted animals. Starting nearby on the wall to the left and curving away into the half-light is a row of irregularly placed red, black, and yellow horses, cattle, deer, and other figures including an imaginary creature called in French a *licorne*. Some of the animals are done in solid colors; others appear in outline only. Straight ahead at the end of the chamber are four huge black bulls, the largest of which is about eighteen feet long.

But the trouble with any description of individual figures is that it loses the effect of the whole, the first flood of impressions as your eyes sweep over the paintings and your mind tries to take in the entire chamber. There is the same problem of how much your eye can hold during the rest of the guided tour. Next comes the Painted Gallery with red and black horses and cattle on the ceiling, and just beyond an iron bar that you are not allowed to pass is the figure of a great black falling horse; then comes the Main Gallery with bison and more horses and a frieze of swimming deer.

I took the guided tour twice. But later I requested and received permission to go past the iron bars into places

Only a few human figures have been depicted in cave paintings. One is pictured in this Lascaux mural: a man with a bird's head falls backward, having been killed by a charging, wounded bison; below him is a bird on a post.

usually closed to tourists. One morning an hour before the ticket office opened, I was admitted to the cave. I turned right just before the entrance to the Main Gallery, maneuvered through a narrow cleft in the limestone, and climbed down a ladder into a pit more than twenty feet deep. Turning around at the foot of the ladder, I saw the strangest of all the Lascaux pictures. To the extreme left in black outline is a rhinoceros, and to the right is a large bison, head and horns lowered as if charging, with spears or arrows penetrating deep into its body. Directly in front of the bison's horns is a crude stick-figure of a man falling over backwards, mortally wounded by his prey. The man is wearing a bird-head mask, and just below him is the figure of a bird set on a pole.

The meaning of prehistoric pictures like these is still being debated. I will merely pass on what Bordes told me: "Let me tell you my story of this painting, a science-fiction story. Once upon a time a hunter who belonged to the bird totem was killed by a bison. One of his companions, a member of the rhinoceros totem, came into the cave and drew the scene of his friend's death—and of his revenge. The bison has spears or arrows in it and is disemboweled, probably by the horn of the rhinoceros. This is how it was."

That scene had been viewed in the morning, but the best time to see Lascaux is at night after the tourists have left. Then you can spend several hours in the cave. You can stand and look leisurely and imagine prehistoric artists at work. They must have had scaffolding of some sort to get at the ceilings and upper walls. They painted by the light of torches and lamps, a number of which have been found in the caves. The lamps are round flat stones hollowed at the middle, with animal grease in the hollows and grooves on the edges where wicks may have rested.

When you move about and play your flashlight over the painted surfaces, you begin to appreciate the artists' genius. Figures which appear relatively flat and static when seen by fixed lights suddenly bulge out at you in three dimensions among moving lights and shadows. And at the end of the Main Gallery you stoop under another one of those iron bars, crawl through a tunnel into the Chamber of Felines, and find more art work. In a cramped little alcove off the tunnel is an engraved horse and three engraved catlike animals, one with seven darts in it. You can crawl on past more alcoves and a trench several feet deep toward the tunnel's end, which is an impassable fissure blocked with clay.

Until his death in 1961, Abbé Henri Breuil of France was a leading world authority on prehistoric art. He had thoroughly investigated the French caves, making tracings himself of many of the engravings and paintings. In the above portrait by Charles R. Knight, Breuil is posed before le Moustier in 1927, garbed and equipped for a search. At right he is shown outside Lascaux in 1940 talking with the boys who had just discovered the cave.

Lascaux has yet to be fully explored. Hundreds of people visit there every day, and although some digging goes on, it is impossible to conduct large-scale excavations under these conditions. The present entrance is an enlarged version of the hole through which the four boys clambered back in 1940, seeking their lost dog. But that was only an accidental cave-in. The original entrance has never been discovered, although some prehistorians suspect that it may lie somewhere past the Chamber of Felines and beyond the place where clay blocks the tunnel.

There is more art of about the same era in the Valley of Caves at two famous sites on the road to Combe Grenal: Font de Gaume and Combarelles. Many of the paintings in the Font de Gaume cave are faded or obscured under mineral crusts deposited by seeping water. You have to make at least three or four visits before your eyes can follow the faint curving lines, ignore the gaps and obliterations, and make out the magnificent shaded and polychrome mammoths, bison, reindeer, and other animals. You will also understand why authorities state that Font de Gaume must have been even more impressive than Lascaux before water seepage did its damage. The nearby Combarelles cave includes a narrow, twisting corridor almost a thousand feet long which, according to a recent estimate, contains about four hundred engravings, mostly of horses—although there are also paintings of bison, bears, mammoths, oxen, reindeer, and men.

About twenty other caves and shelters in the area contain further examples of prehistoric art, and there are some forty other sites in the rest of France and thirty more in Spain. An exact count is difficult to make. For one thing, records of past discoveries may be buried in obscure journals, and new discoveries are being made every year or so. One of the most recent finds occurred in the Spanish village of Nerja on the Mediterranean coast when five boys sneaked into a ravine to share a forbidden cigarette. Suddenly a bat flew out of a hole in the earth. The boys dug their way in, and another cave was added to the growing list.

Abbé Breuil visited Lascaux soon after the boys discovered the cave. Here with one of them he views the imaginary beast the French call a licorne. Archaeologists are not sure of the exact date of Lascaux but estimate it between the late Perigordian and early Magdalenian periods. Above, at top, is a painting of a wolf from Font de Gaume; below it is a bison from Niaux.

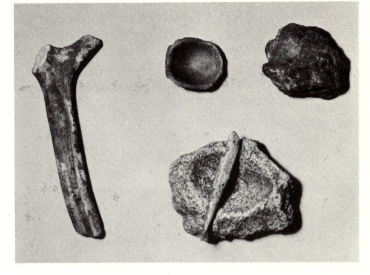

At left are two many-colored bison from the cave of Altamira in northern Spain. At right is the equipment of the cave painter: a mortar and pestle (bottom) used for grinding up the pigments; a bone painted with a yellow or red earth-pigment called ocher; a shell container for ocher; and a scraper to blend and soften the color after it was applied.

Before all this evidence had accumulated, however, the experts denied the authenticity of cave art as violently as they had once contested the nature of Neanderthal man —and for roughly the same reasons. According to that prevailing attitude, the most advanced creatures short of modern man himself were apes or near apes incapable of creative work of any kind. That attitude was so strong people simply did not bother to think about the things they saw with their own eyes. For example, during the early 1800's tourists frequently visited the Niaux cave in the French Pyrenees, and one of the guides to the cave pointed out paintings of extinct animals as part of his conducted tour. He also reported the existence of the paintings to a museum. Yet no one took seriously the findings at Niaux or at other sites—another example of the fact that we see only what we are prepared to see.

The first man to look at prehistoric paintings and recognize them for what they were was less fortunate than the Niaux guide. The guide was merely ignored. But Don Marcelino de Sautuola, a Spanish nobleman and an amateur archaeologist, was ridiculed and even accused of fraud. One summer day in 1879 he was digging in the Altamira cave, which had been discovered on his estate ten years earlier—again, as in the case of Lascaux, during a search for a lost dog.

He had dug there often, looking for stone tools and other prehistoric remains. His twelve-year-old daughter, Maria, was with him, as she had been many times before.

TEXT CONTINUED ON PAGE 100

Some of the beasts that both threatened Upper Paleolithic people and gave them their food parade past in this rhythmic painting of a frieze at Font de Gaume. A bison with a great humped neck (above) is superimposed upon a small horse, which extends beneath. At left is a mammoth with curved tusks.

LIMESTONE SHELTER

HARPOON

COLORED PEBBLES—P. 136

THE SORCERER—P. 110

IVORY HORSE—P. 109

HARPOON—P. 111

LAUREL- AND WILLOW-LEAF POINTS—P. 104

HANDPRINT—P. 101

VENUS OF SIREUIL—P. 118

BISON ENGRAVING—P. 19

LAUSSEL VENUS—P. 18

HERBERT S. BORST

AN UPPER PALEOLITHIC TREASURY

If many of the long-hidden Upper Paleolithic treasures seen in this book, everything from cave paintings to pierced sticks, had been found in the earth layers of one imaginary shelter, a cross section of the layers would look like this sketch. The lowest (oldest) layers are the Perigordian and the Aurignacian, in which art such as the sculpted head on page 106 was found. Next above is the Proto-Magdalenian ("proto" means first), which was similar to the more abundant Magdalenian period. Sandwiched in between these two is the Solutrean culture, which has yielded elaborate points, or spear tips. The top culture layer represents the mysterious Azilians and ends the Upper Paleolithic period.

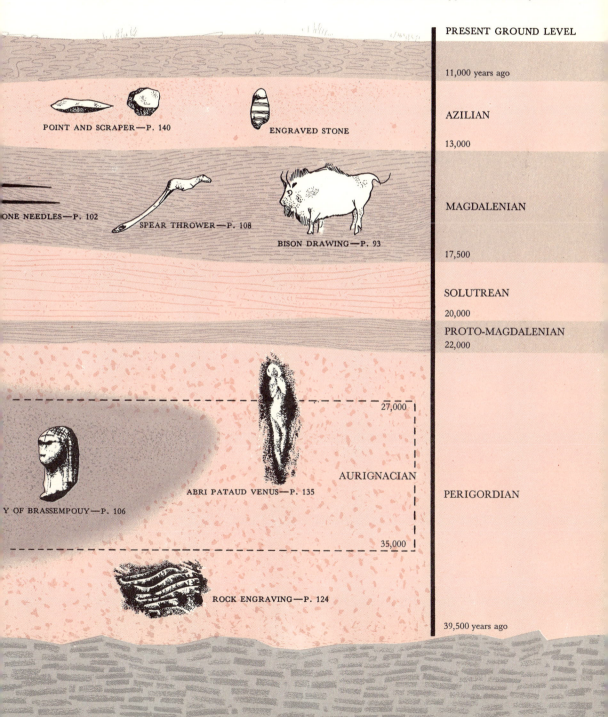

PRESENT GROUND LEVEL

11,000 years ago

AZILIAN

13,000

MAGDALENIAN

17,500

SOLUTREAN

20,000

PROTO-MAGDALENIAN

22,000

POINT AND SCRAPER—P. 140

ENGRAVED STONE

ONE NEEDLES—P. 102

SPEAR THROWER—P. 108

BISON DRAWING—P. 93

27,000

AURIGNACIAN

35,000

PERIGORDIAN

ABRI PATAUD VENUS—P. 135

Y OF BRASSEMPOUY—P. 106

ROCK ENGRAVING—P. 124

39,500 years ago

TEXT CONTINUED FROM PAGE 95

But on this occasion, holding a candle in her hand, she happened to look up at the ceiling of a side chamber. She cried out at what she saw by the flickering light: *"Toros! Toros!"* Maria was wrong in one respect. They were not bulls but a group of more than twenty red and black bison and other animals arranged in a superb fresco.

Don Marcelino found engravings and further paintings, and he published an account of Altamira the following year, attributing the work to prehistoric artists. But most authorities, led by the great French prehistorian Émile Cartailhac, were convinced that the Spanish amateur was deceiving himself or them (an artist had been staying with Don Marcelino at the time the cave was discovered). Furthermore, they refused to come and see for themselves. There the matter stood until fifteen years later when another French prehistorian reported cave paintings and engravings in France at la Mouthe cave near les Eyzies. Within the following decade cave art was recognized at Combarelles, Font de Gaume, and other French caves. Cartailhac publicly confessed his error, and the existence of prehistoric artists has not been seriously questioned since then.

The challenge now is to understand the artists and the cultures of which they were a part. At this point we are concerned with the human evolution that took place from about 40,000 to 30,000 years ago—and immediately we have another major mystery. What happened to the Neanderthal people of Combe Grenal in France, and in Europe generally, during the first five millenniums of this period? According to Bordes, the Neanderthal tribe that developed tools such as backed blades may have evolved into modern men, becoming our ancestors. Many other prehistorians believe that different kinds of men evolved elsewhere and entered Europe as migrants or invaders, probably from southwest Asia.

By either theory there must have been clashes of some sort between more advanced and less advanced peoples. The Neanderthals disappear rather suddenly at many sites where their final layers lie immediately beneath layers representing more advanced kinds of human beings. Perhaps a proportion of the Neanderthals were absorbed into the new groups by interbreeding. But it seems likely that most of them struggled to preserve their way of life—and failed. History has many such tragic and bitter episodes.

Fossil remains show that the Upper Paleolithic people who supplanted the Neanderthals were like modern man

At the cave of Pech Merle, located southeast of the Valley of Caves, is this panel of horses and handprints from the Perigordian and Aurignacian periods. The two horses were drawn in broad black lines and spotted in red and black. Their hind legs overlap, and remains of a red line-drawing can be seen. The very clear hand impressions were made by outlining in black.

in body and brain size. Their works suggest a mental capacity no different from ours. But a fuller understanding of the cave painters and their art cannot be reached until a number of less spectacular things have been analyzed.

The cave painters, and other early men as advanced as they, developed an enormous variety of tools. They brought about a golden age in which materials other than stone were also used for artistic purposes. They were not the first to make wood and bone implements, but the evidence of those implements is particularly abundant at this time.

This evidence also implies a rich variety of ways of life, of hunting methods and customs. Archaeologists investigating layered deposits speak of five major Paleolithic cultures, which have been named after various sites and regions (Perigordian, Aurignacian, Solutrean, Magdalenian, and Azilian). For example, the Solutrean culture is named after the site at which it was first recognized in the village of Solutré near Lyon in southeast France. About thirty such sites have been discovered in the Valley of Caves.

Like our other ancestors of the late Ice Age, the Solutreans hunted reindeer chiefly. They did paintings and engravings but were most outstanding as stoneworkers. They produced long, slender, and exquisitely flaked flint tools, notably "laurel-leaf" and "willow-leaf" points worth thousands of dollars each to collectors. These people may also have been the first to learn the craft of sewing. The earliest-known needles with eyes come from their sites, which indicates that they dressed in fitted clothing.

The Solutreans first appeared about twenty thousand years ago and existed as a distinct culture for only two or three thousand years. This culture, like all others, was shaped by certain factors: climate, natural resources, and the psychological and social characteristics of human beings very much like ourselves. But the specific nature of those factors—for example, what actually happened to encourage exceptional stone working—is the sort of thing which prehistorians are trying hard to learn.

Other modern-looking men whose tools were not quite so richly varied followed the Solutreans and played an even more prominent role in European prehistory. Along

The Solutreans were probably the first to sew clothing, but the Magdalenians were better tailors; they used the bone needles shown above.

At right are two famous Lascaux paintings of deer. At top are deer heads sketched in black that have been explained as a herd crossing a stream—the heads just above water. This drawing technique was used continuously in the cave art of all periods. Below is a small red deer with fantastic antlers.

a bend in the Vézère River about two miles from les Eyzies is the isolated rock shelter of la Madeleine. During the past century this site has yielded a wealth of material including tools and weapons made from bones, antlers, ivory, and stone. There are forked lance-points, polishers, engraving tools, or burins, a variety of fine needles and harpoons, and spear throwers made of long flat bones which with a sharp flick of the wrist can propel projectiles. (Until recently use of similar throwers was widespread among the Australian aborigines and other primitive tribes today.) Many of the tools have engravings on them.

The Magdalenians, who are named after this site, achieved the most advanced culture of any people that had yet settled in the valleys of the Vézère and the Dordogne. Their culture lasted for more than 4,000 years (between 17,500 and 13,000 years ago) and was preceded by a group of people so similar that they are called Proto-Magdalenians (First Magdalenians--see chart on pages 98–99).

An imaginary visit to one of these settlements would contrast in many ways with the previous visit to a Neanderthal site. For one thing, the Magdalenian settlement is more spread out to provide space for more numerous

These slender points, or spear tips, about five inches long, were made during the Solutrean period. The points shown above are rippled on one side like willow leaves. (The first is smooth, being the reverse side.) Laurel-leaf shapes (at right) are chipped on front and back sides.

activities and for two or three hundred persons instead of thirty to fifty. The faces of the people and the words they use are not familiar to us, of course. But we recognize gestures and expressions and intonations, for these human beings are our kind. Brought up in the twentieth century they would behave the way we do, and we would behave as they do if we had been reared in a prehistoric environment. In a fundamental sense we are at home here at their shelters.

Women work in and around skin tents set up beneath the overhang of the shelter. They are sewing and repairing clothes, scraping skins stretched taut on the ground, cooking and tending fires. They and the men wear necklaces of shells and pierced teeth, and pendants of bone engraved with the figures of reindeer and other animals. Cosmetics are common; by far the most popular color is red, which is obtained from the mineral earth known as ocher. This pigment is used to paint the faces of the dead as well as the living, a custom passed on from Neanderthal times or earlier (and still prevalent in our times, although today we apply rouge instead of ocher).

A stoneworker has finished trimming a large flat-topped core of flint into a rough cylindrical shape. He sets one end of an antler against the top edge of the flint, strikes the other end with a hammering stone, and produces a long thin flake. Placing the antler in different positions along the rounded side, he strikes off one blade after another, spiraling in toward the center of the core in a sort of peeling or unwrapping procedure. He is making blades by a method which yields an estimated thirty-five feet of cutting edge for every pound of flint worked, as compared with about three feet yielded by the techniques of his Neanderthal predecessors. Later, using other tools made by different methods, he will groove shafts of wood and bone to haft some of the blades.

The Magdalenians had probably mastered basic stoneworking techniques as completely as had the Solutreans. But as a rule the Magdalenians' tools were made merely to do a job, for they were plain and utilitarian, without elaborate flaking. These people directed their esthetic energies to the engraving of bones, ivory, and antlers—and, above all, to cave art. Many of the most striking paintings at Font de Gaume, Altamira, and a number of other sites are their creations. Their works represent the peak of a tradition that had been developing for a period of at least 13,000 years.

What is the significance of the cave art, and why did

These Sandia points were made by Indians of New Mexico. Resembling the European points opposite and crafted in a similar fashion, they are around 8,000 years old.

TEXT CONTINUED ON PAGE 108

SCULPTURE OF THE CAVE ARTISTS

Although the cave artists of Upper Paleolithic times are most famous for their colorful and lively murals, they also deserve to be remembered for their sophisticated sculpture. Both the head at left, which is named the Lady of Brassempouy, and the stopperlike object below left were carved in ivory during the Aurignacian period. The tiny head (about an inch and a half high) was carefully sculptured to emphasize the details of the lady's peculiar headdress. Later, particularly in the Magdalenian period, sculptors became more interested in decorating objects than in carving figures. The carved animal below is typically Magdalenian; it may have been the decorated part of a weapon. The boy's head etched into the flat stone is also Magdalenian. On the following pages are shown other art objects from this fruitful time when early man first discovered the various uses of art.

ALL: MUSÉE DES ANTIQUITÉS NATIONALES; PHOTOS BY HURAULT

These figures show the Magdalenians' fascination with animals: a bison with head turned (top); a horse at the tip of a spear thrower (above); and a magnificent three-inch-long horse sculptured out of ivory.

TEXT CONTINUED FROM PAGE 105

it flower when Upper Paleolithic men arrived? We can only speculate about the answers to such questions, but some of the speculation is based on reasonably solid ground. It is clear that the Magdalenians and their predecessors must have been driven by exceedingly powerful forces in their search for suitable sites. Unless you are compelled by fear or other strong reasons, you do not go deep underground through crevasses, pits, and tunnels where you have never been before and where you can easily lose your way in the blackness.

I remember following the route which prehistoric artists had followed thousands of years ago in one small French cave. The entrance was a hole in the side of a rock, a hole just about big enough to squeeze through head first. Then I found myself flat on my stomach in a slit of a passageway so low that I could not raise my head more than a few inches without bumping it against the ceiling. I had to

keep my head close to the damp, mud-covered floor and
move along by wriggling snake fashion because handgrips
were few and far between and my feet slipped away behind me in the mud.

Every foot of the way I was hoping to reach a place
high enough to stand up in. But there was small comfort
when it came—a narrow grotto with a jagged pit leading
to deeper and wetter passages below. I had to pass along a
muddy, slippery ledge at the very edge of the pit. Then
there was more crawling through low limestone passages
until I came to the "art gallery," a grotto containing engravings of bison, a reindeer, a mammoth, and a horse's
head. The distance from the entrance to the gallery is only
about a hundred yards, yet it took more than half an hour
to get in and another half hour to get out.

Our ancestors must have had some particularly pro-
found compulsion to burrow into such a place, although

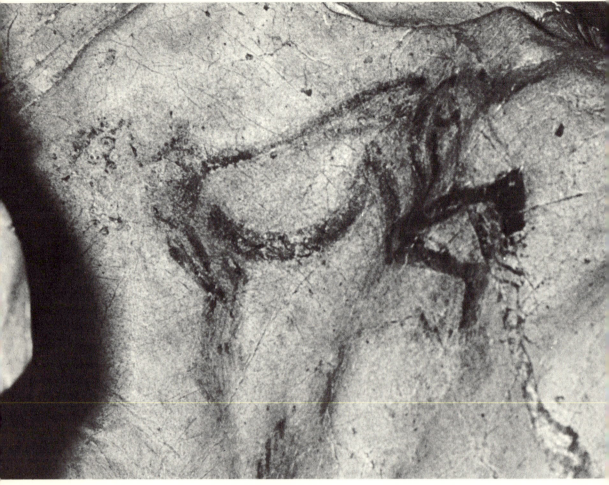

In the cave of les Trois Frères in the French Pyrenees is this engraving of an extraordinary, manlike figure called the Sorcerer. According to Abbé Breuil, whose reconstruction is at right, this Magdalenian figure was the god of that cave; his function was to control the abundance of game. The figure has large round eyes, the ears of a stag, and two thick antlers. Such details as hands and a kneecap were carefully engraved.

110

that cave is simple and not particularly dangerous. The stamina and courage required to get through the labyrinths of much larger and more complicated caves is awesome, even for present-day explorers who are equipped with portable searchlights, special clothing, and other gear. Yet this is what those early men did, and they probably did it for the sake of their beliefs. All the evidence suggests that they were seeking secret places for the practice of magic and of religious ceremonies.

One cave in the French Pyrenees has a remote chamber which contains two bison modeled in clay and an engraving of a harpoon; in the center of the chamber is a little clay hillock. You can practically see prehistoric people performing a dance around the hillock. Their footprints, preserved in clay, are everywhere. In another cave nearby there is a kind of sanctuary, a narrow niche including the figure of a man with antlers on his head, bear paws, and the tail of a horse. The figure, known as the Sorcerer, is located in a position which is extremely difficult to get at—twelve feet up on a wall that dominates the floor below. It is as if the figure were suspended above an altar.

The atmosphere of secrecy is heightened by the fact that cave artists often preferred almost inaccessible surfaces for their work. Furthermore, they did not hesitate to draw figures directly over figures previously drawn by other artists. As a matter of fact, in many cases you find confusing tangles of lines representing many levels of superimposed drawings. Apparently there was nothing sacred about the figures themselves; they were not regarded as masterpieces to be preserved for all posterity. What seems to have had special significance is the location of the pictures on selected parts of wall surfaces.

Beyond this we can only infer the intimate relationship that existed between the people and the animals of prehistory. They were tied to one another by invisible but very real bonds. The animals moved according to instinctive patterns of their own, patterns of day and night and changing seasons. Men moved with them, observing and maneuvering and coming in for the kill when the time was right. Hunter and hunted were caught up together in a great natural rhythm, thinking and watching together.

It is no wonder that out of the many thousands of individual paintings and engravings practically all depict animals. The very rare representations of human beings are generally crude by comparison. Men probably identified themselves closely with wild animals, so closely that

MUSÉE DES ANTIQUITÉS NATIONALES: PHOTO BY HURAULT

Above is a Magdalenian barbed harpoon made of a reindeer antler. It was either hafted on a javelin or projected by a spear thrower.

they must have believed they could influence the behavior of their prey—by incantations and dances and ritual drawings. In a practice reminiscent of voodooism, they may have made figures with spears stuck in them to try to bring about death by remote-control magic.

The rise of art is one phase of the spectacular evolutionary spurt which occurred toward the end of the last glacial period. The existence of similar styles and similar painted figures at sites hundreds of miles apart implies communication among distant groups, perhaps in the form of great meetings like those held by tribal confederations among the American Indians. And that in turn implies that a major factor in the advancement of modern man was the establishment of laws and taboos and punishments and priests and chieftains. Early man's society was becoming more and more complicated, a sure sign of his cultural evolution.

Before a hunt, men like the hunters pictured above probably gathered in a sanctuary to pray for success. At right is a rendering of a cave painter at work on one of the mysterious animal murals. In his left hand he holds the hollowed-out stone that contains his pigments; with his right hand he applies color with a bone scraper. He wears sewn garments of hide and fur.

A canopy shields the Abri Pataud excavation where scientists are finding traces of Paleolithic men.

VI

DIGGING AT THE ABRI PATAUD

Near the town of les Eyzies is a brilliantly organized excavation which could serve as a model of how archaeology should be managed. It also tells much about how future questions regarding early man may be answered.

The site lies on the flank of the town's prominent landmark, the great limestone cliff against which the les Eyzies Museum of Prehistory is built. You can see it on the slope of a hill from the road that winds through the town and across the Vézère River and on into a countryside where traces of the distant past are abundant.

The excavation is known as the Abri Pataud—*abri* is the French word for shelter, and Pataud is the family name of the farmers who owned the site in the nineteenth century. After a thorough survey of some 150 possible sites in southern France, this shelter was selected in 1949. The choice was made by one of the world's foremost investigators of prehistory, Hallam L. Movius, Jr., Professor of Anthropology at Harvard University. Movius has an encyclopedic knowledge of his field, which calls for a far wider range of information than most scientific disciplines.

He can describe in detail the flint-working technique of primitive tribes (and is equally well acquainted with the skills of English craftsmen who are still making gunflints for muskets, carbines, and horse pistols). He is also able to converse expertly on such subjects as Canadian caribou, whose migration habits resemble those of the reindeer hunted by our Stone Age ancestors, and the best way to search for a new site and the chances of finding one.

More important, Movius is known for his coordinated approach to the study of prehistory. During the past thirty years he has worked increasingly with geologists, botanists, chemists, sociologists, and other specialized investigators.

One of the first discoveries at the Abri Pataud was a young girl's skull (above). Its exact location in an earth layer was noted by means of vertical and horizontal measurements. Scientists then tested the charcoal in the layer and determined that the child had lived about 20,000 years ago.

115

This is an unfinished and continuing project. The site is rich in remains of our direct ancestors, people who looked and behaved just like us, though they lived under different conditions. Digging has been under way for more than four years and has reached a maximum depth of nearly twenty feet below the original ground surface. Half a dozen layers have already been exposed. They contain a great many artifacts and represent the period from about 34,000 to 20,000 years ago. The exploration of still deeper levels will require at least two more seasons; analysis of the findings still goes on. Indeed, it may be ten years or so before we have the full report of the Abri Pataud.

There are good reasons for such intensive and painstaking work. The main objective is to miss as little as possible, to extract every available bit of information from the earth, an objective which has not always guided investigators of the past. As a matter of fact, truly scientific digging is a relatively recent development. For many years people misinterpreted and twisted the evidence of prehistoric tools to fit in with their conviction that human beginnings extended back only a few millenniums at most. Early in the eighteenth century a 100,000-year-old hand axe, picked up in a London gravel pit, was identified as a spear point used by early Britons against a Roman army invading Britain in A.D. 43.

This explanation, by the way, at least recognized the hand axe as something made by men for a specific use. But most theorists of the day were not ready to concede the point that the hand axe had any particular function. They saw nothing purposeful in the flints that were dug up. According to a widely held notion, the finely patterned flints were accidents, freaks of nature, like figures seen in wave-battered sea cliffs or in sandstone eroded by wind—perhaps these newly found fragments were merely bits of rock that had been shattered during violent storms by bolts of lightning or earth movements.

Today we have an intense interest in and respect for the relics of prehistory. Yet it once required considerable fortitude to go against the spirit of the times and recognize the facts in the face of contemporary beliefs. The first man to put himself on record with the correct interpretation was an English antiquarian, John Frère, who found flint hand axes twelve feet below the surface in a Suffolk clay pit. Realizing that the artifacts antedated Rome and Greece and all familiar civilizations, he wrote in 1797: "The situation in which the weapons were found may attempt us to

Professor Movius, at right, works over a table in his laboratory at the Abri Pataud. Here he analyzes each find and records the data. Below, he is shown in his office-laboratory at Harvard University.

The stone farmhouse at left was once the home of the Pataud family. It now serves as a laboratory for Professor Movius' staff while digging is in progress. The century-old house stands against the cliff some fifty feet from the excavation. Two workmen lounge at the doorway.

The discovery of art objects, such as the stone statue of the Venus of Sireuil (right), was the hope of many early cave investigators.

refer them to a very remote period indeed; even beyond that of the present world."

These remarks made little impression. Only the sheer weight of accumulating evidence could bring about a change in perspective, and as always happens sooner or later, the evidence did accumulate. One of the most important developments came about fifty years after Frère's statement with the work of Jacques Boucher de Perthes, a French customs official who apparently found his job highly uninteresting. In any case he tried his hand at writing political pamphlets, music, poetry, and plays—none of which created a stir among his contemporaries.

Boucher de Perthes attracted more attention as an amateur archaeologist. Working at a site near Abbeville, a town located at the mouth of the Somme River on the French side of the English Channel, he collected many flint implements. The gravelly soil also yielded the remains of extinct subtropical species of elephants, rhinoceroses, and saber-toothed tigers. In 1846 he made his position quite clear: "These rude stones prove the existence of man as surely as a whole Louvre would have done." But it was not until 1859 that his and similar finds received official approval from a special British investigating committee.

Archaeology still had its troubles, however. In fact from one standpoint the troubles were more serious after flints were recognized as a scientific clue to early man. People ignorant of the existence of prehistoric toolmakers had no reason to be especially interested in caves and rock shelters. But as soon as the facts became known the treasure hunt was on. There are few things as powerful as human

TEXT CONTINUED ON PAGE 123

In 1907 the Dordogne shelters were visited by treasure seekers (below), but digging into prehistory did not become scientific until the 1940's.

BOTH: PEABODY MUSEUM, HARVARD UNIVERSITY

From all the possible sites in the Valley of Caves, the Abri Pataud was chosen for extensive excavation because of a careful investigation that had been made there in 1953. Professor Movius suspected that the site might yield more Paleolithic riches than any other rock shelter in France. In the summer of 1958 the area was cleared for scientific excavation. The trees and the surface debris were removed from the slope (above), and a horizontal grid of pipes was built out over the working area. From the pipes, vertical lines were let down to the ground, and the entire site was marked off in two-meter squares. Guided by this measuring system, Movius' students began digging trenches (right), keeping track of all objects found in the culture layers. Each layer, representing one occupation of the shelter by a migrating group of Paleolithic people, yielded a distinctive number of tools and flints. The archaeologists concluded that the richness of the Abri Pataud was not in its art but in the striking individuality of its many culture layers.

120

TEXT CONTINUED FROM PAGE 119

curiosity and the desire for easy money, and farmers, shop-keepers, and adventurers came out in droves seeking productive sites. They often found what they were looking for —and did incalculable damage, particularly in France.

One dealer in flints for tourists had a simple and direct technique. He would enter a cave, put his lantern on the floor, dig up a shovelful of dirt and dash the contents against a convenient wall. If he heard the sharp click of flints striking the wall, he would pick up the lantern and start looking for implements. Another worker blasted earth and rocks with dynamite so that he could get more material quickly, and at one large site amateurs even brought a plough and a team of horses into the cave.

Unfortunately, amateurs were not the only offenders. Archaeologists themselves have been guilty of the "museum" approach to prehistory. They often went after objects of art exclusively, venus figurines and bone and flint tools decorated with engravings. In the process of obtaining such pieces they rummaged among but rejected thousands of less impressive items, plain tools which would hardly attract curators accustomed to the delicate vases and jewelry of classical times. In the back of some caves I have found fine examples of Neanderthal and Magdalenian craftsmanship discarded by past investigators who might have known better.

In short, many workers were considerably more interested in loot than in learning. They regarded prehistoric caves as open and unprotected territory ripe for repeated raiding. They thought of living sites as buried collections of individual artifacts, each of which could bring a high price on the market place. Of course, as far as basic knowledge about early man is concerned, this attitude could not have been further from the truth. No single piece, however unusual or beautifully shaped, means much by itself. It may show that one of our ancestors had great stone-working skill, esthetic talent, or an advanced sense of design—but this leaves us no wiser than before, for such qualities have been known for years.

Actually a living site is a complex unit, a kind of mosaic in three dimensions. Every piece of rock or bone, worked or unworked, is significant chiefly by virtue of its specific position in relation to all other pieces. Remove it without first

PEABODY MUSEUM, HARVARD UNIVERSITY

This vertical rod shows the depth of the Abri Pataud excavation. The lowest level is 20 feet down.

As gingerly as a detective would look for fingerprints, the archaeologist cleans a skull. Here he scrapes dirt from the eye socket with a penknife.

123

recording that position precisely, and its basic meaning is destroyed. Checking up on the discovery of a new star, a new species, or a new mineral deposit may be relatively straightforward. But once a site has been completely excavated, the excavator's record is all that remains. Archaeology is the only science in which you destroy your evidence forever in the process of obtaining it.

Many sites in the Valley of Caves, including some of the most famous ones, have already yielded their works of art and have been ruined as far as scientific investigation is concerned. Poor digging means irretrievably lost information, and poor digging has been the general rule. Among sites involving Paleolithic people the Abri Pataud is an outstanding exception to this rule, just as Combe Grenal represents an exception for the study of Neanderthal people.

Every step in the Abri Pataud excavation, the location of every test trench and carefully plotted square, is part of an elaborate and thorough plan conceived by a master de-

One of the few art objects unearthed at the Abri Pataud is a rock with a snakelike, or serpentine, engraving. This design may have been carved at the same time some of the Lascaux cave murals were being painted nearby.

tective. Movius has organized things so that the site will yield the maximum evidence possible considering our present state of knowledge, and the data continue to pile up as digging proceeds. His laboratory, one part of a farmhouse built into the ancient cliff shelter, has a wooden cabinet containing thousands of file cards—one card for every flint implement found so far at the site. Each card describes a piece, its size and function, special remarks about how it was made, the depth at which it was found, its position along east-west and north-south coordinates. Other file cards indicate such details as the position of pieces in relation to one another and the contours and extent of various layers and sublayers.

It is slow work brushing dirt away a bit at a time, continually keeping track of the color, texture, and grain size of the soil, and stopping frequently to measure the positions of flints and take stock of the situation. Some times eight persons digging all day long will excavate only a few inches

At the site a sculptor prepares a plaster cast of the snakelike engraving. Rather than transporting the heavy rock from the shelter, a cast is made for laboratory study. The meaning of the engraving is not presently known.

Paleolithic man depended on reindeer for food and shelter. His lean-tos and clothes were made from the skins. Out of antlers and bone were carved spear points and art objects. Left, a graceful reindeer was engraved on the cave wall at Combarelles. At right, hunters carrying game return to the hearth of their shelter.

MAURICE WILSON; BRITISH MUSEUM (NATURAL HISTORY)

deep in an area not much larger than the surface of a billiard table. The method requires a great deal more patience than the bulldozing tactics of the not so remote past, when a worker considered his day wasted if he could only gouge out a single trench forty or more feet long and three to four feet deep.

But the patience pays off. To take one example: slow and systematic work has revealed a number of unusual features in the lowest layer excavated to date at the Abri Pataud. This layer, representing the second of the five cultures of Paleolithic men to come to the valley, is called Aurignacian II. These people, who preceded the Solutreans and Magdalenians, were the creators of some of the earliest prehistoric art. Most of the Aurignacian II layer is confined to a small area of the site, a kind of natural basin located in the back of the shelter where evidence of human occupation occurs in a fantastic concentration. It contains some twelve hundred tools and a complex system of overlapping hearths, one of which is of particular interest.

The blackened fireside, exposed after several days of digging, is beautifully preserved. Furthermore, one ob-

A hearth was found in one of the Abri Pataud's lower layers (above). In a higher layer three kinds of engraving tools, or burins, were identified. Both sides of the burins are shown at right; arrows point to distinctive notches.

servation has confronted Movius and his co-workers with an as yet unsolved mystery. On one side of the hearth is a group of burins, or engraving tools, of a special type, and about a dozen end scrapers lie directly opposite on the other side. The problem is to figure out the meaning of this simple and clear-cut pattern, which remains as it was set up, and then left, by people who lived thousands of years ago. Did two craftsmen sit close together merely because it was night and they were using firelight to work by? Or were they both working on stages of the same task, and if so, what were they making? Or is there some totally different explanation?

The hearth is significant for another reason, one which illustrates how the nuclear physicist can help the archaeologist. Hendrik de Waard of the University of Groningen in Holland has visited the site and studied pure, concentrated ash from fires that once burned in this living layer. The ash contains C-14, a radioactive form of carbon which disintegrates at a regular rate and acts as a kind of atomic clock to help us determine how old the material is. According to de Waard's findings, the hearth is about 34,000 years old. This date is older than dates that had previously been obtained for the Aurignacian II culture— some 4,000 years older. This probably means that all of the other dates for early man should also be adjusted. Apparently he evolved more slowly than was previously thought. So the study of a single hearth changes our concept of prehistory.

There are many other intriguing problems at Movius'

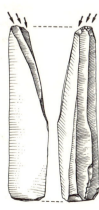

PIERRE LAURENT

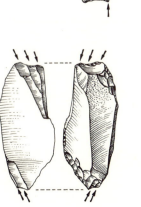

site: for instance, the matter of burins. These engraving tools are found by the thousands in some layers. They are as common as razor blades, having obviously been used frequently and for some simple everyday purpose. Investigators have a hunch that the burins may have been used chiefly in constructing wooden implements, such as shafts for javelins. Yet it seems unlikely that so many burins would have been needed merely to make javelin shafts. This observation leaves us with the same question: What were the people at the Abri Pataud making, apparently in very large quantities?

Yet this is only one part of the burin problem. The people made a great many different kinds of burins, perhaps fifty or more distinct types in all—each designed to produce a groove of a different size or shape. Present-day woodworking craftsmen also have a large and complicated assortment of engraving tools to make furniture, sliding drawers and doors, cabinets, and other such civilized items. Whatever their products, it seems strange that the woodworkers needed such a variety of burins.

Furthermore, the people seem to have made widely different things at different times. One type of burin, making up nearly a fourth of all burins found near the bottom of a certain living layer, almost disappears by the time you reach the top part of the layer—while another type of burin previously little-used appears in large quantities. Obviously techniques were changing markedly, but we do not know why, or what objects were being made. But these changes need not reflect radical transformations in traditions or customs, because they may occur within a single cultural layer representing many generations of continuous occupation by closely related tribes. And animal bones in the layer indicate that during all the time hunters were going after the same game, so food-getting methods and the climate could not have changed much either.

Thus we find riddles in the numbers of tools, and we are given hints at the activities of the people who made and used the tools. And the more clues we find, the more complete will be our understanding of how our ancestors lived. More than 25,000 flint implements have already been gathered at the Abri Pataud, and perhaps twelve to fifteen times as many chips that represent waste material left by the toolmakers.

There are also number patterns in materials besides flint. About thirty crates of animal bones and bone fragments and teeth—mostly from the widely hunted reindeer

TEXT CONTINUED ON PAGE 134

130

Traces of the once-abundant reindeer, such as the antlers at left, have been found in the shelter's layers. The precise location of a find is recorded (below) as staff assistants carefully measure its position.

A reindeer and some small game are being roasted on a crude spit that has been fashioned from tree branches.

In the background, a man and a woman carry bundles of sticks while a hunter, spear in hand, shoulders his catch.

MAURICE WILSON

TEXT CONTINUED FROM PAGE 130

—await further examination by paleontologists. Another specialist is concerned with quantities of mollusk shells, which are abundant in only one of the cultural layers and are pierced, probably for stringing together into necklaces and other ornaments. The shells appear to have come from both the Atlantic and the Mediterranean coast, 100 to 150 miles away, indicating that the people either obtained shells from traders or else sent out expeditions of their own. Botanists trained in the study of ancient plants are making examinations of samples of fossilized pollen which will make it possible to deduce what trees grew during various periods and how climates may have changed. Geologists will obtain related information from detailed analyses of soils.

The Abri Pataud has also yielded a remarkable object of art, a real museum piece. It was found late one summer afternoon in 1958 after a heavy rainstorm had caused a small erosion in one corner of the site and had dislodged a rock about the size of a grapefruit. One of Movius' students casually picked up the rock, turned it over in her hand, and suddenly saw a beautifully shaped bas-relief figure. It was a prehistoric venus, a woman depicted with her arms missing (a common feature of such figures), carved more than 20,000 years ago. The venus was important to the excavators, but no more so than a new pattern of flint instruments would have been.

So work proceeds at the Abri Pataud. Evidence continues to accumulate, and a great deal more may be expected during the months and years ahead. There are further layers, older layers, which may lie ten to fifteen feet below the lowest level excavated to date, layers which may well take us back to Neanderthal times and perhaps to even more remote periods. Every inch of the digging will involve the same precise, thorough, and voluminous record keeping and will require consultations with specialists in a wide range of scientific fields.

Furthermore, as Movius emphasizes, this is only one site. Other undisturbed living sites will have to be found and excavated and ultimately the results compared with the Abri Pataud before we obtain a more complete and sophisticated picture of how prehistoric people lived in southern France during Paleolithic times.

This delicately carved venus was made over 20,000 years ago by an artist of the Abri Pataud. It is the most important art object yet found there.

134

MUSÉE DES ANTIQUITÉS NATIONALES:
PHOTO BY HURAULT

VII

PHOTO BY CHARLES HURAULT

DEATH OF THE HUNTER

Early man has been observed coming into the Valley of Caves and flourishing there. Leaving his African origins far behind, shucking his apelike form and his subhuman habits, he evolved into modern man during the course of 200,000 years. In the valley he achieved an amazing record, which includes some of the most impressive and significant developments in the entire course of human evolution. Seventy centuries before recorded history, prehistoric men and women were burying their dead here, wondering about life and life after death, creating rituals, and expressing themselves in works of art.

The story of early man began with geological slowness, but then it started to reel faster and faster. During that initial phase, the trend of man was gradually upward, advancing toward increasingly complex and sophisticated ways of life. The second phase however was quite different; a spectacular, relatively sudden change took place. For some five millenniums, from about 17,000 to 12,000 years ago, Upper Paleolithic people such as the highly creative Magdalenians flourished in southern France and elsewhere. That was prehistory's golden age. It was a time of highly skilled and versatile hunters, the period of the artists who created the greatest paintings and engravings of Lascaux and Font de Gaume and Altamira.

Now we come to more somber twilight times. The pulse of evolution skips a beat; the bottom seems to drop out of things as one of the greatest of prehistoric cultures is changed into a pathetic and puny way of life. Something tragic has happened to the last of the Magdalenians and to their scattered descendants.

Their fate is written in a language whose letters are buried bones and flints, but it is just as obvious as if the general facts had been spelled out in plain English. You

At left is the mouth of the vast cavern of Mas d'Azil. Brightly striped and spotted Azilian pebbles (above) were found in a cave inside the cavern.

137

can tell what happened by examining the record. The archaeological layers of the Magdalenians are almost always thick, and they cover wide areas and stretch far out in front of caves and rock shelters, often to the very edges of rivers winding through the valleys. It is clear that these people frequently lived and worked at considerable distances from the protecting walls of cliffs, as if they were powerful and self-assured and, in the words of François Bordes, ". . . feared nothing—neither men nor animals."

Directly on top of these ample layers are layers representing the descendants of the Magdalenians, generations of "frightened people." They are the so-called Azilians, named after the Mas d'Azil cave in the French Pyrenees where initial excavations were conducted some seventy-five years ago. The Azilians did not range over much of Europe, and the layers commemorating them tend to be thin and restricted in area; as a rule they are confined mainly to the rearward parts of shelters. These people apparently spent most of their at-home time huddled under rocky overhangs with their backs literally to the wall.

Furthermore, they generally avoided the chief sites of the Magdalenians, as if they felt that such impressive sites were not for the likes of them. We may imagine that they revered and perhaps worshiped the artists and hunters who were their ancestors. Certainly they moved into some sites where their ancestors had lived, but usually into the smaller shelters such as past hunters might have used for temporary camps and stopovers during extended trips. It appears that while the Magdalenians had settled in groups of perhaps two hundred to three hundred persons, the Azilians lived in scattered bands of perhaps a dozen members. More often than not they chose out-of-the-way settlements, little caves in hidden valleys.

Other evidence confirms the same impression: man's horizons in the time of the Azilians were somehow shrinking; there was less security and less confidence. The Azilians were not great innovators. Most of the flint implements which they commonly used had been developed during late Magdalenian times. Also, their tool kits were smaller and less varied.

If an archaeologist finds sixty different types of tools and weapons in a Magdalenian layer, he will be lucky to find half as many types of stone implements among the remains of the Azilians. Their bone tools are also less varied and fewer, and less beautifully worked.

But by far the most dramatic sign of the change is the

One of the mysteries concerning Magdalenian culture is why so many of the weapons had pierced tips. At far left (above) is a pierced and engraved stick, and at left is the top part of another stick that was decorated with two bison heads. At far left (below) is one explanation for the hole: a Magdalenian leader wields a stick by putting his thumb through it. This theory is so widely accepted that the pierced sticks are generally called batons. Many mysteries also surround the later Azilians, whose shelter was so big that today a two-lane highway runs right through it (above).

139

Some of the cutting tools used by the Azilians were short scrapers (top) and stone points. The tools above, and the pebble at right engraved with the head of a wolf, were found at Mas d'Azil.

apparent disappearance of all traces of cave art. The Azilians left pebbles, generally flattish, painted in red and black (see page 136) with a variety of stylized forms —rows of dots, parallel strips, ladderlike and cross-shaped patterns, and bands with scalloped edges. These objects are found in large numbers and certainly had a special meaning—a meaning which remains a mystery. Perhaps, as has been suggested, the markings are symbols of religious or magical significance. Eduard Piette, who originally identified the Azilian culture late in the nineteenth century, saw even more significant possibilities in the colored forms on the pebbles. He thought they might be pictographs and the crude beginnings of an alphabet.

In any case, as examples of art these painted pebbles are a long step down from the glory of the Lascaux wall paintings. As far as we know, the Azilians never engraved animals on tools and the walls of caves, and they never created great paintings or sculpture. Perhaps while taking refuge in certain caves they saw and admired the works of their ancestors, but there is no evidence that they did anything more than that. Art vanishes from the record, and with it a world disappears. A culture which had been established by people essentially like ourselves and had apparently been built on firm foundations was gone.

We know the main reason for the passing, and it is a strange one. Disaster does not always come with a bang, in the form of epidemics or famines or floods. Sometimes a simple change of climate is sufficient, and this is just what happened in the Valley of Caves. Indeed, the climate actually changed for the better. Glaciers retreated, and snow and ice melted, bringing more temperate conditions, and that was enough to disrupt an entire way of life.

The approach of disaster may be observed through the evidence gathered at sites along the Vézère River—notably at the first site of the Magdalenian culture, the great la Madeleine rock shelter itself. An analysis of animal bones in one of the upper archaeological layers shows signs of subarctic local climates. The record includes remains of the chamois, the snow partridge, and the pika, a cold-weather.type of hare. But by far the most abundant remains are those of reindeer. This particular layer dates back some 13,500 years ago to a time when southwestern Europe was a hunter's paradise. It was in that very period that reindeer herds were most numerous and widespread, extending south of the Pyrenees mountain range and even to the Mediterranean coast.

MUSÉE DES ANTIQUITES NATIONALES: PHOTO BY HURAULT

This fragment of bone engraved with two ibex heads was also discovered in the cave at Mas d'Azil.

141

All this can be inferred from the next-to-top layer at the la Madeleine site. Then trouble comes in the uppermost layer. Reindeer are scarcer, and the red deer and the wild boar make their appearance for the first time—signs of good hunting are hard to find. The next stage is represented clearly at the Abri Villepin, another rock shelter on the banks of the Vézère not far from la Madeleine. Now in an Azilian layer the reindeer has practically disappeared, and red-deer populations are markedly on the increase.

The rise of the red deer is only one clue to the change in climate, but it fits in with other observations. This animal is a forest dweller, as contrasted with the open-tundra reindeer. The glaciers were melting back toward the north, and herds of reindeer followed them and moved away from the Valley of Caves as the climate became warmer. Studies of fossilized pollen reveal that pine, birch, and juniper trees were being replaced by trees typical of denser and more widespread forests: oak, hazel, alder, elm, beech.

There is probably plenty of food about, since animal populations are still large. But the environment is quite different. Forest animals do not go about in herds whose

ZDENEK BURIAN

Reindeer, once the chief target of Magdalenian hunters (left), had almost vanished at the time of the Azilians. In their warmer climate the Azilians fished and hunted and tracked the red deer of the forest. Deer and salmon were carved on the antler section above at the end of the Upper Paleolithic period.

patterns appear to the eyes of the weary hunter like dark and solid islands in oceans of snow. Forest animals are camouflaged and travel in small groups; they hide effectively in undergrowth and wooded glades and move as swiftly and silently as shadows.

So the problem is not adverse conditions, but changing conditions. And change, operating on people unaccustomed to it, can be disastrous. Prehistoric man begins to depend to an appreciable extent on the comings and goings of an inferior species. Generations and generations of reindeer hunting establishes traditions so deep-rooted that when the reindeer leave, adjustment is difficult and only partly successful—and a great culture collapses utterly.

Certainly some of the hunters followed the reindeer north. To do so, however, they had to desert countrysides that had been home for centuries and live less settled, less secure lives. In any case, many of the people stayed behind, and their numbers dwindled during Azilian times. And their spirit dwindled too.

The dwindling was tragic enough in itself. Yet it had

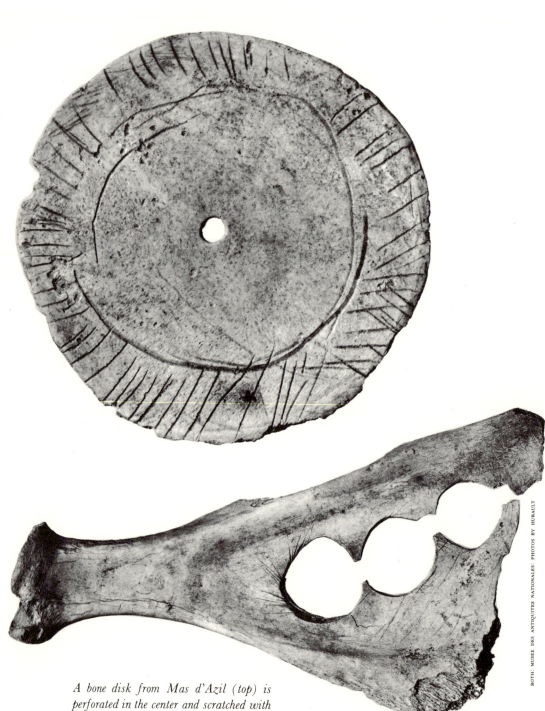

A bone disk from Mas d'Azil (top) is perforated in the center and scratched with short straight lines around the edges. It may have been used as a clothes button. The disk is actually half the size pictured here and was originally carved from the flat part of a bone like the one above.

even more serious overtones. It seemed that the future was limited not only for the descendants of a once-mighty breed of men in France but for all men everywhere, for all time. The point is that apparently there was nothing that could stop similar disasters from occurring again and again and again.

People who live strictly on what the wilderness happens to offer, on the wild plants and animals that exist in a particular region, cannot expect long-term security. They will always be ruled by the unpredictable forces of nature. Their fortunes will always prosper or fail to prosper depending on whether natural conditions become more or less favorable. So man seemed destined to depend completely on events beyond his control. An observer of the world as it was eleven or twelve thousand years ago could hardly be blamed for taking a dismal view of man's prospects as a species, at least if he judged by the turn of events in southern France.

But things were happening elsewhere in the world that would save man from such a brutish destiny. At this stage of prehistory the spotlight shifts to the Near East. Here developments were under way which were to play a major role in bringing Europe out of its cultural doldrums. We are looking now at the people included in a two-thousand-mile arc that takes in parts of present-day Iraq, Iran, and Turkey. These people, who lived far from the Valley of Caves, were not producing such spectacular works as the cave paintings. Like the Azilians and other European groups, they were far too busy going after every available source of food and learning to exploit the land more and more intensively. The big difference in the Near East was that local conditions favored the most radical change yet to occur in the human way of life, the rise of agriculture.

The world's earliest farms were probably small areas reserved for the protection and care of selected plants and animals some eleven thousand years ago. Then, about two thousand years later, village communities were organized. They were crude settlements that obtained a significant proportion of their food from domesticated beasts. After such communities were established—so different from the foot-loose tribes of earlier times—there could be continuing and controllable food surpluses. Populations soared, and there was time for mulling things over and for new inventions and new specialties. Soon the first cities appeared, the first kings and dynasties were established in the valleys of the Tigris, Euphrates, and Nile

The hunter slowly became a farmer as Europe's weather became more moderate. He no longer depended upon wild animals for his existence and could now feed upon vegetation and learn the rudiments of agriculture. The clay figure of a boar (above) was made in Iran at about the time of the Azilians and was perhaps used as a fertility symbol.

DR. R. J. BRAIDWOOD: ORIENTAL INSTITUTE, UNIVERSITY OF CHICAGO

TEXT CONTINUED ON PAGE 148

145

TENTS, BOX SCORES, OR SYMBOLS?

Near the end of a side gallery off the main chamber of the Lascaux cave is the strange scene at left: two sketchy ibexes glare at each other over a grill-shaped object; another one of the straight-lined objects is seen above a group of small horses at far right. What do these squares mean and what is their relationship to the hunters and artists of the late Upper Paleolithic period? A well-supported guess is that the squares are tectiforms—tent-shaped designs representing dwellings constructed by early man. Abbé Henri Breuil, however, believed that the shapes were coats of arms; a number of them have indeed been quartered and colored so that they look like knights' shields. Some of the equally puzzling figures below, which were found painted on the walls of the Spanish cave of el Castillo, could be shields; others might be hunting snares—or possibly even trees. Then there is the theory that the tectiforms may have been drawn to tell a story by means of symbols or to help the hunter keep score of his killings. New speculations will be made as more knowledge about the cave artists becomes available. But it is unlikely that modern man, despite all his fascination with symbols and ciphers, will ever surmise the true meaning of these designs or be able to decode the message of the colored pebbles in the cave of Mas d'Azil.

TEXT CONTINUED FROM PAGE 145

rivers. Ultimately came the great invention of writing; with writing came the end of prehistory.

Eventually Europe inherited agriculture and civilization from the Near East, and the descendants of the Magdalenians and Azilians were among the inheritors. From that time on the story of les Eyzies and the surrounding countryside becomes part of the pageant of Western civilization; the nations of Europe slowly form, battles are fought, and freedoms are won. These developments are the concern of the historian, and many of his problems are exceedingly formidable. But the remaining problems that confront the prehistorian are even more difficult. Without the benefit of written records of any sort, he is trying to deal with roots and beginnings, with the first people to believe in gods or spirits and to conceive ideas and symbols and rituals.

The tension, the excitement, of prehistory lie in the continuing search for answers to critical questions. The investigator is always looking for more evidence along familiar lines and for new kinds of evidence. He is searching for ways of dating the past more precisely, for new types of tools or constellations of tools, new living-floor complexes indicating the work of specialists or specialized activities, new caves and new art-sites, and new sanctuaries. Above all, he is looking for the unexpected, which is certainly one of the most challenging aspects of research activity in all branches of science.

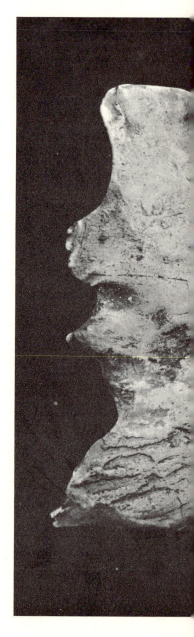

We would like to know a great deal more about the origins of prehistoric peoples, particularly the Neanderthals; to gain this knowledge, scientists must make comparisons between Combe Grenal and other sites. Now we view the Neanderthals as if through unfocused lenses; the general shapes are there for all to see, but the details are blurred. A central problem is to understand why men began burying their dead and why the practice seems to have been pursued chiefly by one of the Neanderthal groups. And there are many other problems. How did art arise from Paleolithic rites, and why? Why did it flourish particularly in certain parts of France and Spain? What specifically were burins and other tools used for, and how can we account for changes in the types of tools used by people whose environment seems not to have changed significantly?

Answers to many of these questions lie buried, waiting to be found, in the known sites and unexplored shelters of the Valley of Caves.

*It is difficult for us to understand
the story that the prehistoric engraver
of this reindeer antler wanted to tell.
But the Magdalenian symbols are all
there for us to interpret—a man between two horses' heads (above) and a
thick serpent between horizontal lines.*

Mr. Punch's Almanack, 1882

An 1882 cartoon satirized Darwin's theory of man's evolution.

AMERICAN HERITAGE PUBLISHING CO., INC.

James Parton, *President*

Joseph J. Thorndike, Jr., *Editorial Director*

Richard M. Ketchum, *Editor, Book Division*

Irwin Glusker, *Art Director*

HORIZON CARAVEL BOOKS

RUSSELL BOURNE, *Editor*

Janet Czarnetzki, *Art Director*

Mervyn Kaufman, *Assistant Editor*

Judith Harkison, *Chief Picture Researcher*

Lucy Davidson, *Picture Researcher*

Elaine K. Andrews, *Copy Editor*

Mary Gloyne Payne, *Editorial Assistant*

Gertrudis Feliu, *Chief, European Bureau*

Claire de Forbin, *European Bureau*

ACKNOWLEDGMENTS

The Editors are deeply indebted to Professor Hallam L. Movius, Jr. of Harvard University and to Professor François Bordes of the University of Bordeaux, France, for their generous cooperation in helping to prepare certain portions of this book. Special thanks are also owed to Dr. Louis Leakey, Curator of the Coryndon Museum, Nairobi, Kenya, and to Leonard Grant of the National Geographic Society. The Author wishes to express his special gratitude to the Wenner-Gren Foundation for Anthropological Research for a grant which made it possible to visit the les Eyzies region and participate in excavations there. In addition, the Editors are grateful to the following individuals and organizations for their assistance and for making available material in their collections:

André Varagnac, Chief Curator, Musée des Antiquités Nationales, St. Germain-en-Laye

Mme. Marthe Chollot-Legoux, Assistant Chief of Research, l'Ecole Pratique des Hautes Etudes, Paris

Lucy Knight Steel, New York

British Museum (Natural History), Department of Anthropology

American Museum of Natural History, New York

Chicago Museum of Natural History

BBC School Publications

Special research and photography: New York—Geoffrey Clements; France—Charles Hurault; England—Susanne Puddefoot, Maureen Green, Derek Bayes; Italy—Maria Todorow

Special drawings by Maurice Wilson, Pierre Laurent, David Greenspan, and Janet Czarnetzki

FURTHER REFERENCE

Readers interested in digging more deeply into prehistory may visit several institutions in this country and abroad where fossils, flints, or other cultural traces from ages past may be viewed. Among them are:

American Museum of Natural History, New York

Chicago Natural History Museum

Peabody Museum of Archaeology and Ethnology, Harvard University

Princeton University Museum of Natural History

University of Pennsylvania Museum

Arizona State Museum, Tucson

Cleveland Museum of Natural History

Denver Museum of Natural History

Los Angeles County Museum

Musée de l'Homme, Paris

Musée des Antiquités Nationales, St. Germain-en-Laye

les Eyzies Museum of Prehistory

British Museum (Natural History), London

For those who wish to read more about prehistory, the following books are recommended:

Bandi, Hans-Georges. *Art of the Stone Age*. Crown, 1961.

Bataille, Georges. *Lascaux: Prehistoric Painting*. (Skira) World Pub., 1955.

Boaz, Franz. *Primitive Art*. Dover, 1955.

Braidwood, Robert J. *Archaeologists and What They Do*. Watts, 1960. *Prehistoric Men*. Chicago Natural History Museum Press, 1957.

Breuil, Abbé H. *Four Hundred Centuries of Cave Art*. Sapho, 1952.

Burkitt, M. C. *Old Stone Age: A Study of Paleolithic Times*. New York University, 1956.

Coon, Carleton S. *The Story of Man*. Knopf, 1962.

Dart, Dr. Raymond A. with Denis Craig. *Adventures with the Missing Link*. Viking, 1961.

Douglas, John Scott. *Caves of Mystery*. Dodd, 1956.

Eiseley, Loren. *The Immense Journey*. Random, 1957. *Darwin's Century*. Doubleday, 1958.

Goldman, Hannah and Irving. *First Men: The Story of Human Beginnings*. Abelard, 1955.

Graziosi, Paolo. *Palaeolithic Art*. McGraw-Hill, 1960.

Greene, John C. *Evolution and its Impact on Western Thought: The Death of Adam*. Mentor, 1961.

Leakey, L. S. B. *Adam's Ancestors*. Harper, 1960. *The Progress and Evolution of Man in Africa*. Oxford University Press, 1961.

Lucas, Jannet M. *Man's First Million Years*. Harcourt, 1941.

Mellersh, H. E. L. *The Story of Early Man*. Viking, 1959.

Movius, H. L., Jr. *Three Regions of Primitive Art*. University Pub., 1961.

Oakley, Kenneth P. *Man the Tool-Maker*. University of Chicago Press, 1959.

Peake, Harold and Fleure, H. J. *Hunters and Artists*. Oxford University Press, 1927.

Raphael, Max. *Prehistoric Cave Paintings*. Translated by Norbert Guterman. Pantheon, 1945.

Rostand, Jean. *The Orion Book of Evolution*. Orion, 1961.

INDEX

Bold face indicates pages on which maps or illustrations appear